Richard Ira Sugarman

Rancor Against Time: The Phenomenology of 'Ressentiment'

RICHARD IRA SUGARMAN

RANCOR
AGAINST TIME:

The Phenomenology
of 'Ressentiment'

FELIX MEINER VERLAG
HAMBURG

CIP-Kurztitelaufnahme der Deutschen Bibliothek

Sugarman, Richard Ira:
Rancor against time : the phenomenology of
"ressentiment" / Richard Ira Sugarman. —
Hamburg : Meiner, 1980.
ISBN 3-7873-0456-8

In Memory of My Father, Albert Sugarman

and My Teacher, John Wild

TABLE OF CONTENTS

PREFACE

A.

This book explores the ontological meaning of the phenomenon of 'ressentiment'. The word "ressentiment" became a technical term of philosophy with the publication of Friedrich Nietzsche's 'On the Genealogy of Morals' in 1888. In 1912 Max Scheler set forth, in 'Ressentiment', what has remained to date the only philosophic work exclusively devoted to elaborating the investigation Nietzsche set in motion. The concept that is attached to the technical term "ressentiment" was, for Scheler, pregnant with great philosophic significance, because: "Among the scanty discoveries which have been made in recent times about the origin of moral judgments, Friedrich Nietzsche's discovery that *ressentiment* can be the source of such value judgments is the most profound."[1] However, with Scheler's first published work, being the last word in a muted dialogue that spanned only the last twelve years of the nineteenth century and the first twelve years of the twentieth, the discussion of the "most profound" of recent discoveries concerning the formation of judgments of value was closed.

It was not until 1954, in 'What is Called Thinking?', that Martin Heidegger, without citing Scheler and without using the term "ressentiment", reopened for philosophic questioning the radical, ontological character of Nietzsche's original reflection upon the phenomenon captured by the term "ressentiment". An unstated implication of Heidegger's treatment of Nietzsche, a theory which the thesis of this book sets out to demonstrate, is that Scheler's phenomenological description of 'ressentiment', by moving strictly within the ontic realm, has prematurely served to foreclose the deserved exploration of its ontological dimension.

The purpose of this book is to develop the essential structures of a phenomenological ontology of 'ressentiment'. It is systematic rather than historical in character. We shall use Scheler's work to clarify the phenomenological project of describing the concrete, patterned appearances of the phenomenon in the life-world of contemporary existence. We shall move towards the exploration of Heidegger's fundamental ontology in order to secure the original philosophic discovery of Nietzsche against Scheler's covering over of its genuine ontological dimension. At the center of inquiry will be our own reconstruction of Nietzsche's project, still presenting a challenge to contemporary philosophy.

B.

The sense of the French noun "ressentiment" is clearly captured in its lexicographic formula: "The remembrance of an injury and the desire to avenge same."[2] Scheler has offered a sound reason for retaining the French word in any philosophic investigation of the phenomenon signified by the term and has also set out a helpful, if most provisional, elaboration of its meaning:

"We do not use the word 'ressentiment' because of a special predilection for the French language, but because we did not succeed in translating it into German. Moreover, Nietzsche has made it a *terminus technicus*. In the natural meaning of the French word I detect two elements. First of all, *ressentiment* is the repeated experiencing and reliving of a particular emotional response reaction against someone else. The continual reliving of the emotion sinks it more deeply into the center of the personality, but concomitantly removes it from the person's zone of action and expression. It is not a mere intellectual recollection of the emotion and of the events to which it "responded" — it is a re-experiencing of the emotion itself, a renewal of the original feeling. Secondly, the word implies that the quality of this emotion is negative, i.e., that it contains a movement of hostility."[3]

While the English noun "resentment" possesses marked similarities to the French word "ressentiment", Scheler's characterization of the phenomenon specifically rules out the employment of the two wards synonymously. The English verb "to resent" derives from the same Latin prefix and verb as "ressentir". However, the English verb permits, even mandates employment when the subject is said merely "to feel or show displeasure at (a person, act, remark, etc.) from a sense of injury or insult"[4].

Absent from general English usage is the sense of time-lag between offenses suffered and displeasure or indignation expressed. As characterized by Scheler, the very expression of "resentment" would serve to preclude the origination of the phenomenon of "ressentiment".

For, present in the former concept and absent in the latter are: 1) an expression of displeasure and indignation; 2) a recognition of the occasioning injury or insult contemporary with its appearance; 3) the absence of a desire for revenge, or, more precisely, the non-necessary character of the desire for revenge. 'Ressentiment', on the other hand, must manifest both a desire for revenge and the blockage and subsequent postponement and sublimation of that same desire.

Nietzsche, in his own characterization of 'ressentiment', positioned the bottled-up desire for revenge between the source of its origination and the end at which it aimed:

". . . every sufferer instinctively seeks a cause for his suffering; more exactly, an agent, still more specifically a *guilty* agent who is susceptible to suffering — in short, some living thing upon which he can, on some pretext or other, vent his affects, actually or in effigy: for the venting of his affects represents the greatest attempt on the part of the suffering to win relief, *anaesthesia* — the narcotic he cannot help desiring to deaden pain of any kind. This alone, I surmise, constitutes the actual physiological cause of *ressentiment*, vengefulness, and the like: a desire to *deaden pain by means of affects*."[5]

The spirit of revenge is a strategy designed to produce anaesthesia, to alleviate the source of human suffering, "to deaden pain of any kind". "Ressentiment" is the name Nietzsche gives to the complex structure which begins with human suffering and aims at its anaesthetizing. The desire for revenge at the center of 'ressentiment' searches for a "guilty agent" to explain the nature of suffering for which no reason or justification is given. When the desire for revenge is stymied its expression is altered but its intention remains the same, thereby venting its affects in effigy.

C.

Scheler's work demonstrates how the structure of 'ressentiment' informs the meanings of the sphere of interpersonal life, and how this results in the deforming of man himself. The founding assumption that governed Scheler's phenomenology of 'ressentiment' was the belief that the source of human suffering is always perceived as originating from the other person.

Scheler believed that he had carried to successful completion the work that remained to be done in the service of Nietzsche's discovery.

He wished only to correct Nietzsche's position that Christian love (*agape*) was a sublime expression of 'ressentiment'. On the contrary, Scheler argued that *agape* represented the solution to the existential problems issuing from the phenomenon of 'ressentiment'.

Nietzsche's thought is still represented by Heidegger as focusing "deliverance from the spirit of revenge". However, the spirit of revenge is not representely solely, or governed fundamentally, by our relations with other persons, as Scheler had believed. Heidegger states:

"Revenge, for Nietzsche, is the will's revulsion against the passing away and what has passed away, against time and its 'It was'. The revulsion turns not against the mere passing, but against that passing away which allows what has passed to be only in the past, which lets it freeze in the finality of this *rigor mortis*."[6]

Our own enquiry will focus on the phenomenological path leading to and beyond the spirit of revenge directed against time.

In approaching the spirit of revenge directed against time, we shall want to ask how, and why, Scheler overlooked the ontological dimension of the phenomenon, and what he represented as the solution of the problem. We shall want to know how and why Nietzsche described the spirit of revenge directed against time itself. We shall want to ask after Nietzsche's professed solution to this problematical phenomenon, the two-fold doctrine of eternal return and the overman. Moving beyond the spirit of revenge against time, we shall present a reflection on the ultimate metaphysical horizon within which the rancor against time itself moves and ask after the conditions that have governed its interpretation. We shall conclude by sketching a way open to overcoming the rancor against time.

D.

The main philosophic vehicles transporting us along the path of our investigation are Dostoevsky's 'Notes from the Underground', Scheler's 'Ressentiment', representative selections from Nietzsche's writings, with special emphasis on 'Thus Spake Zarathustra', and two of Heidegger's works, 'Being and Time' and the essay 'Time and Being'. The systematic structure of the thesis, its method, and order of presentation are as follows:

1. Following Plato's counsel for conducting a philosophic enquiry

we open with a picture of the phenomenon under investigation. 'The Notes from the Underground' provides us with a vivid image (*eikasia*) of the lived-experience of 'ressentiment' in the person of Dostoevsky's strange man from the underground. Just after he had completed 'On the Genealogy of Morals', Nietzsche expressed upon reading the 'Notes from the Underground': "the instinct of kinship . . . [that] spoke up immediately; my joy was extraordinary".[7] In Chapter I, we shall show the unique character of Dostoevsky's portrayal of an emblematic life that moves within the existential matrix of 'ressentiment'.

2. The image, however, is not yet the phenomenon. It is highly unstable and lacking the regularity of patterned structures which the concrete appearance of a phenomenon possesses in its manifold variations. The shifting tangle of "lived-experience" must be purified by phenomenological description so that it can be clarified at the level of *logos* or interpretation.

Max Scheler's 'Ressentiment' provides an indispensable vehicle for a phenomenological investigation that enables us to trace the silhouette of the formal, eidetic structures of 'ressentiment'. Removing the phenomenological brackets from the elicited eidetic structures of 'ressentiment' permits the image to emerge as a concrete, ontic phenomenon which makes its patterned appearance in the life-world of contemporary existence. However, in order to make the ontic appearances philosophically comprehensible, the unitary ground governing the possible appearance of the phenomenon must be exposed.

3. The phenomenology of 'ressentiment' is rendered ontological when the Being of the phenomenon is disclosed. The Being of the phenomenon is revealed by demonstrating the manner in which it has become what it is. The matrix of Nietzsche's thought provides the vehicle for demonstrating the historicity of 'ressentiment' as disclosed in the transformative junctures of the inner development of philosophy.

The historicity of the phenomenon shows what remains constant in the philosophic tranformations undergone, and the ontological structure of the rancor against time itself. The fulcrum for exposing the unitary ground of the abiding structure of rancor against time is Nietzsche's central work, 'Thus Spake Zarathustra'.

The ontology of 'ressentiment' bequeathes a task to philosophy which Nietzsche's own professed solution to the problem, the two-fold doctrine of eternal return and the overman, fails to meet — deliverance from the rancor against time. The task is metaphysical in character, for it must re-examine the founding premises that would lead to an overcoming of the rancor against time.

4. Heidegger's 'Being and Time' provides a framework for understanding the metaphysical legacy of the problematical phenomenon of 'ressentiment', the transcendental conditions governing any possible appearance of the phenomenon. 'Time and Being', Heidegger's late published essay, opens the horizon through which the phenomenon can be thought through, and breaks a path stretching towards its resolution.

I. 'RESSENTIMENT' AS LIVED-EXPERIENCE: DOSTOEVSKY'S MAN FROM THE UNDERGROUND

A. Philosophical Function of the 'Notes from the Underground'

Dostoevsky's 'Notes from the Underground' offers an endless source of existential content challenging philosophical interpretation at almost every turn in the self-presentation of a life lived out with fastidious self-awareness. Relieved of the demands for philosophical self-criticism and justification, it offers a powerful description of the phenomenon which this book sets out to clarify conceptually, i.e., the phenomenon of 'ressentiment'.

Playing a unique role within the corpus of Dostoevsky's writings, the 'Notes' serve as a microcosm of western man's experiment with the project of becoming human in a world that yields reluctantly to his understanding. Just as man stands ready to fulfill the will of an old testament, i.e., to take possession of the earth, at the same hour in which technology is prepared to liberate man from all that is burdensome in the task of sustaining life, Dostoevsky's man from underground ruminates on the consequence of elevating the demands of security so high as to make prosperity incompatible with human freedom. In an age when happiness is promised to man simultaneously with his insertion into the world, the man from underground asks after the price to be paid for such happiness. Just as man has begun to become calculable, predictable, and completely "natural", the denizen of the underground experiences with full force the existential antimonies that knot together a life that is as aimless and disoriented as it is premeditated and "unnatural".

Many of the themes first introduced by Dostoevsky have been taken up and purified in the sustained and systematic reflection of subsequent existential philosophy. Even as the underground man anguishes over the loss of existential meaning, phenomenologists, beginning with Husserl, have come to reflect upon philosophic problems involved in describing the constitution of meaningfulness. Just as the underground man inveighs that it would sometimes be better "if two and two did not equal four", thereby suggesting that reason has become divorced from existence, we recognize that philosophers in the continental tradition, again beginning with Husserl, have inaugurated a sustained investigation into the primary world of the senses that anchors and informs conceptual reflection. And, where the imaginary author of the 'Notes' broods over the loss of human freedom in an age when the star of technology is beginning to ascend, the problem of human freedom for contemporary existential phenomenology has become to secure an authentic human freedom in the face of the increasingly materialistic thrust of the latest scientific achievement.

If we are content to carve out from the rich detail of the 'Notes from the Underground' those passages which are suggestive of restrictively defined philosophic content, we shall have to acknowledge that the man from the underground resembles the poets whom Socrates describes in Plato's 'Apology' in that he, like the poets, is unable to explain, upon demand, the source of his own inspiration[9]. Dostoevsky, creator of the man from underground as well as his "notes", is concerned from the outset to tell us that he is interested primarily in a life rather than an idea, even if this is said by him to be a prototypical life of incessant theoretical reflection. It is imperative, then, to keep in mind that the views of the man from underground are fitted by Dostoevsky within the fabric of the life of his imaginary author. As such, it is the very existence of this man that is held open for critical inspection and demands philosophical interpretation.

Prefacing the 'Notes from the Underground', Dostoevsky explains that it is his purpose to discover the causes and conditions under which this strange man has made his appearance[10]. His answer is revealed in the power of his portrayal of the interweaving aspects of the life and thought of the man from underground. It is here, at this ever renewed encounter between existence and reflection, that Dostoevsky explores the life-world of 'ressentiment'.

The fact that Dostoevsky is the most self-conscious of the great writers of fiction cuts two ways. As a novelist, he presents an image of 'ressentiment' that emerges within the tangled web of lived-experience. The image is not yet an objectified regularity of shapes that would permit a careful delineation of its boundaries and contours. With Plato's counsel in mind, we move from the level of *eikasia* or image to more purified levels of reflection. In doing so, however, we notice something unique about the structure of 'ressentiment' and Dostoevsky's capacity to portray it within the fabric of lived-experience. If Plato is correct, we can expect that as we move up the rungs of the divided line that mirror the perspectives which we assume on the way to knowing, we shall expect that purification of reflection from the level of image to that of perception, to that of conceptualization, and lastly, to the rung of contemplation, should progressively divest the concrete appearance of its particularity and vividness.

It is, however, a fundamental philosophic argument of this book that the self-transcending character of human existence defies the reduction of Being to meaning, of exteriority to the realm of human intentionality. Moreover, we affirm that the timeless character that reflects the cast of western philosophic reflection always falls short of the timely demands that issue from the perpetually exigent character of existence. It is from this absence of fortuitous convergence that the nature of philosophic 'ressentiment' itself originates ever anew.

We open our reflection with a consideration of Dostoevsky's 'Notes from the Underground' just because it instantiates an essential aspect of the book itself: the apparent incapacity of reflection to subdue and capture existence that transcends the knowing subject.

B. "Out of Joint With the Times and With Time"

The underground man is portrayed throughout the 'Notes' as a man first "out of joint" with the "times" and then subsequently, with time itself. In Part I he images himself as in heroic tension with the current of the times. He is the man who says "no" to the Crystal Palace, the translucent edifice meant to picture the ultimate vision of technological triumph culminating in scientific achievement[11]. The Crystal Palace portrays time that is frozen. Historical time is the horizon within which the laws of nature unfold. Yet, the time of history is closed to a man who understands the laws of nature as inexorable. For the underground man to accept the Crystal Palace's transformation of what passes as historical time he must despair of a future in which his will genuinely makes a difference.

The Crystal Palace symbolizes the world of emerging scientific modernity and the triumph of technology. It is the fruit and issue of the scientific revolution, the philosophy of the enlightenment, and the resultant objectification of man by himself. The emerging social sciences are bringing to a logical conclusion the work set in motion by the natural sciences, to make of man himself a being who is, in every respect, "natural" and, therefore, a being whose behavior is calculable and predictable. Within the context of the 'Notes', it is the world above ground that is represented by the palace of crystal, a utopian image without suffering or strife, but also without freedom or meaning. It is against this world where reason seems to enjoin madness that the man from underground lodges his protest. Just as he as an individual finds himself outside the social world of St. Petersburg, so too does he recognize being human as incompatible with the emerging world of the Crystal Palace. In the theater of his own mind, the underground man seeks to expose the fraudulent appearances that dominate the looks that mandate the choices and activities within the social reality of the *polis*. At the same time, he is concerned with protesting against, and presumably thereby thinking to forestall the ascendancy of the conceptual reflection of western man that has informed the building of the Crystal Palace.

This desire to expose and to protest is given specific illustrations in Part II which chronologically precedes Part I in time. From a psychological standpoint it shows the particular consequences for the underground man of the general theme that time stands still which is presented in Part I. In three decisive episodes Dostoevsky portrays the underground man as time-thwarted. The episodes with the officer[12], with his friends[13], and with Liza the prostitute[14] reveal respectively his inverted relation to public time, the time of filial inter-subjectivity, and the time of eros. The underground man lives in the past because his past is one closed off, i.e., divested of a future. Against Part I every action is disclosed in 'phases'. The phases of time reveal a 'ressentiment' against time in the sense that every present action aims at self-justification of a past perceived as suffering, distortion, and injury at the hands of another. The other, seen from the standpoint of Part II as as a whole, is the self of Part I irreparably injured by time, dispossessed of a future and resentful against time's passage.

Part II, entitled "Apropos of Wet Snow", is a flashback both in the ordinary sense that it recounts events in the past from the standpoint of the present, and in the sense that it provides an occasion for the underground man to relive each of the three decisive events that have shaped his present outlook. His incessant attempts at self-understanding give way in Part II to the recounting of a life of injury and insult experienced at the hands of others. His capacity for brooding over insults, imagined as well as real, and his obsession with avenging them seems limitless.

A police officer quite inadvertently, as the underground man freely admits, had hurried him roughly along in a crowd of passersby and so became the occasion for the underground man to plot revenge against him. For two years, he could think of nothing else. The mere recollection of the occasion drove him to a frenzy. He wrote a novel on the subject. He contrived, at last, after various other strategems had failed, to bump into the officer so that the latter would be forced to recognize the existence of the man he had unknowingly offended. He went into debt to purchase suitable attire for the occasion. At the last moment his plot was foiled as the officer turned in another direction. On the point of despair he was at last vindicated and brought immeasurable, if temporary, happiness when, on the spur of the moment, a rubbing of shoulders takes place.

Shortly thereafter, he runs into his lone friend from secondary school who is on his way to a reunion with some old classmates. The friend is reluctant to take the underground man along no matter how much the latter hints that he would like to be included. The friend's reservations prove to be merited. The underground man manages to sabotage the affair in order to get even with his classmates for refusing to recognize his sensitivity and self-avowed genius. He becomes quite drunk and belligerent, ruins the party, and is asked to leave before he is thrown out.

He staggers outside into the snow where he persists in following the party of classmates to a local house of infamy. Here he experiences the one romantic involvment of his life. He lectures the prostitute Lizavetta on a life of virtue even as he prepares to despise her for the very fact, or so he says, of falling in love with someone so unworthy as himself. When sometime later she comes to visit him, he berates her mercilessly. She leaves, he cries, and so the story ends.

It is in the face of the other that the underground man beholds a recognition of himself. How he appears to others and his concern for recognition at once reveal a 'ressentiment' towards himself in the face of the looks of the others through whose gaze externality penetrates the inwardness of the underground. His sense of the temporality of others is the portal through which he grasps his own self-objectified appearance. He recognizes himself as coveting even the shallow futures of his schoolboy contemporaries and, in so doing, senses more acutely that he is imprisoned by his own self-reflection. In the face of the other, self-justification and integration give way to 'ressentiment' against the other and a life of self-willed appearances in which he seeks power over the other through eliciting the envy of the other in the face of his own contrived appearance.

Even as the looks of the world continually cast withering glances in his direction, he cannot look back except through the process of mediated self-reflection. In the world of action he is left only with the comical possibility of rearranging his own facial expressions. The man who says no to the Crystal Palace because one cannot make a long nose at it is unmasked as a man preoccupied with assuming a dignified expression, above all else, in the face of the other. 'Ressentiment' now turns, at last, underground against all unpremeditated self-expression. To the affective and appetitive drives upon which he insisted in Part I in protest against the laws of reason, he now refuses a future and, thereby, turns these same drives against himself by devaluing their significance. He says 'no' to friendship because it always has the look of falseness and a final and self-arresting no to the other.

The underground man resents a world that he can neither accept nor change. Unable or unwilling to find satisfaction in revenge he has recourse only to spite. The spiteful countenance he turns against other persons, in Part II especially, is directed in Part I against that constellation of forces, agencies, and institutions that define his condition.

C. Suffering, the Absurd, and the Quest for Meaning

Why, then, should we not simply conclude that Dostoevsky's man from the underground is an embryonic presentation of the absurd hero, who finds more adequate, thematic expression in Camus's Sisyphus? In the concluding chapter of the 'Myth of Sisypuhus'[15] Albert Camus presents a trenchant allegory depicting the existential condition of modern man. Walter Kaufmann remarks that the inclusion of the last chapter of the 'Myth of Sisyphus' forms a fitting epilogue to his much used anthology, 'Existentialism from Dostoevsky to Sartre': ". . . as Dostoevsky's 'Notes from the Underground' [may] furnish the best overture, Camus's Myth of Sisyphus, the concluding chapter of his book by that name, is an excellent finale."[16] The unmistakable implication of Kaufmann's remark is that Camus's presentation of the quintessential hero of the absurd represents the final distillation of the outlook expressed by Dostoevsky in the 'Notes from the Underground'. We will now proceed to argue that what Camus commends as the solution to the existential situation of modern man, Dostoevsky diagnoses as the most profound symptom of his malaise. A corollary of this argument, however, is that the stance of Camus's Sisyphus represents a significant stage in the development of the consciousness of Dostoevsky's underground man. Thus the somewhat lengthy analysis of Camus's myth with we will now present will serve to illustrate one moment in the progressive deepening of the underground abyss as well as showing an ultimately aborted resolution of the problem which Dostoevsky, as well as Camus, has considered, but rejected as inadequate to resolve the dilemma of the man from the underground.

The most prominent expression of the inward gaze of the world which appears underground is that of absurdity. The disoriented consciousness of the man from underground invites an immediate comparison with Camus's Sisyphus. Dostoevsky's man from underground shares with Camus's Sisyphus an elemental sense of the senselessness of all pursuits. All meaningful work has degenerated into toilsome labor. The underground man, the retired official, is a man "out of work" in the deepest sense of the word as it harks back to its original meaning in the Greek. He is dispossessed of a work in the sense that he has no *ergon* or function to define and delimit his existence. In the 'Myth of Sisyphus' Camus asserts that consciousness of one's plight is the single recourse from a life fated to meaninglessness. The absurdity of everyday existence is treated as an incontrovertible and universally accepted fact. To be human means to face a life of absurdity. The only way of dealing authentically with such a fate is to unmask the illusion that it could be otherwise. Camus permits this to Sisyphus in the moment of descent, as the rock which he must forever push uphill, rolls back down. In this moment of lucidity Sisyphus would testify to a fate that cannot be surmounted except by defiance of the only kind permitted him, i.e., of an inward sort: "There is no fate that cannot be surmounted by scorn."[17]

The hero of the 'Myth of Sisyphus' alters the meaning of his fate, even if the facts remain the same, by the self-consciously adopted stance which he takes up towards his imposed destiny. Camus's implicit claim is that the interpretation of any given set of facts may be regarded as fact-for-consciousness. The very possibility of meaningfulness presumes the indispensable condition of an intending consciousness. It is the manner in which Sisyphus scorns the hold which the gods exercise over mortals that bears upon our understanding of the condition of Dostoevsky's man from underground. Even in its announced ambiguity, the fate of Sisyphus as described by Camus denies the very possibility of being overturned. Sisyphus, wisest of mortals, is punished by the gods just because he has managed by guile to trick death out of its natural title to his human estate. As Camus describes it, the situation of Sisyphus must be reckoned a hopeless one. Condemned to ceaselessly roll a rock to the top of a mountain, only to see it fall back again each time he brings it to its appointed destination, we must assume that he knows that he shall go on doing so forever. In seeking to escape the self-defining limits of death, Sisyphus earns a fate in which even the sweet release from incessant pain is no longer possible. In other words, death, first understood as an evil which brings to an end the good things of life, is transformed into its opposite, a good which brings the evil sufferings of life to a desired end.

Death, conceived simply as the end of human life, rather than calling attention to the urgency of life and therefore the possibility of philosophy, settles nothing. That Sisyphus comes to this recognition belatedly means that he is denied the chance for tragic action: "If this myth is tragic, that is because its hero is conscious."[18] Only the stance of Sisyphus can be construed as tragic, which is to say "it is tragic only in the rare moments when it becomes conscious".[19] Since the steps leading to a tragic resolution cannot be taken, the tragedy of Sisyphus is a motionless one which Camus describes as "that hour like a breathing space which returns as surely as his suffering, that is the hour of consciousness".[20] The horizon within which his consciousness moves betrays a recognition that the future is sealed as the eternally recurring reflection of the past. Camus impresses upon us the fact that a Sisyphus, hopeful of finding a way out of and beyond his present situation, would render him no longer tragic. "Where would his torture be, indeed, if at every step the hope of succeeding upheld him."[21] The horizon of promise in which the reality of the future could serve to ground the demand for satisfying his earthly aspirations has shrunk to a vision in which the future is understood no longer as beckoning and absent, but rather as nonexistent. Here is the bedrock rationale for ascribing to Sisyphus the role of absurd hero; that is, a hero deprived of deeds and of action. A hero whose knowledge of his situation confers his heroic status simultaneously with his understanding, represents the inversion rather than the expression of the Greek concept of tragedy.

Homer's Sisyphus is tragic because he discovers too late the meaning of overstepping the limits that define human mortality[22]. The tragic flaw of Homer's Sisyphus is his overbearing pride, a which seeks to bear him over the limits of his mortality through tragic action. It is exactly the unknowing pride of Homer's Sisyphus that Camus transmutes into the self-conscious and obdurate scorn that Camus commends as the excellence of the Sisyphus of his own myth. Homer's Sisyphus unknowingly undervalues the consequences of his own defiance. Camus's Sisyphus steals the secret power of the gods more surely than Prometheus. It is he, not they, who shall weigh in the balance the meaning of all human conduct. Not Zeus, but Sisyphus shall become the measure as well as the one who measures the meaning of all things; even of "the things that are, that they are, and of the things that are not, that they are not".[23] His scorn consists in inverting the order of the things that are and the things that are not. Sympathetically rendered, his rebellion consists in the fact, that, to the subjective standpoint of mankind, self-consciously aware of the possibility of freedom, even as negation, he has allotted the power to bestow meaning, even in the face of the superior power of the gods. He is aware of the power which the gods have to torture him. His very awareness, Camus maintains, transforms his torture into a kind of victory: "The lucidity that was to constitute his torture at the same time crowns his victory. There is no fate that can not be surmounted by scorn."[24]

In this same vein, Camus asserts "crushing truths perish from being acknowledged".[25] Self-deception is understood as insincerity. Self-knowledge is identical with self-confession. The fate that can be surmounted by scorn leaves the known facts standing but robs them of their significance. Consciousness is frozen in the present moment. The subject's self-coincidence with his own consciousness replaces the unity of deed and speech longed for in the resolution of classic, tragic action. It is no longer accurate to speak of Camus's Sisyphus as a tragic hero. It is not surprising that he concludes the myth by stating that "one must imagine Sisyphus happy".[26] Happiness is no longer what it was for Aristotle, "the activity of the soul in accordance with *arete*[27]. Rather, it has become what Aristotle expressly rejects, a state of mind.

The meaning of *arete* itself undergoes an inversion. Human excellence is no longer realized in the action called forth by the inner necessity of a given situation; rather, one makes a virtue out of necessity itself. One denies necessity the power to limit human aspiration resulting in a devaluation of both the object of desire and the phenomenon of fated necessity. This phenomenon of making a virtue out of a necessity when the necessity is the source of perceived and un-warranted suffering belongs to the essence of what Nietzsche and Scheler after him called 'ressentiment'. In denying his Sisyphus a righteous anger admixed with his deserved sorrow, Camus conceals the fact of *resentment* even as he initially reveals its expression in the first blush of Sisyphus's recognition of the true character of his fate: "A face that toils so close to stone is already stone itself!"[28] The Sisyphus of Camus yields too soon, even as he demans too much. Consciousness has annihilated the recognition of its own resentment.

If a life of consciousness is inconsequential as Camus paradoxically implies, then consciousness becomes aware of nothing but itself. Yet, he concedes that life cannot be lived always without expectation, even as he warns against the self-deception of hope. The sorrow and the expectation are in the beginning. "Again I fancy Sisyphus returning toward his rock, and the sorrow was in the beginning."[29] With the elimination of the expectation of happiness, the sorrow, too, will disappear. The expectation of happiness, though, is provisionally important in the discovery of the absurd. "One does not discover the absurd without being tempted to write a manual of happiness . . . happiness and the absurd are two sons of the same earth. They are inseparable. It would be a mistake to say that happiness necessarily springs from the absurd discovery. It happens as well that the feeling of the absurd springs from happiness."[30] Only a man who has once sensed the promise of happiness can understand the implication of living without the belief in the power of the gods to bestow its possi-bility. The disappearance of the horizon of promised happiness is not to be confused with the kind of waiting for it, in its absence, which has been associated with Godot. As long as one waits upon the looks of the world for confirmation, a power is invested in the absent but expected reality. There is a dramatic difference between living in the absence of a promise yet to unfold and substituting in its stead a shrunken horizon of a new presence that transforms the previous absence into non-existence. For example, if one believes that the dynamic power of the principle of retributive justice is dormant when one sees wrong committed and apparently rewarded rather than punished, one can still testify to the belief in a principle of retributive justice whose power is not yet manifest. If one concludes that the absence is unbearable and succumbs to the belief that absent justice is illusory, one no longer lives in the atmosphere of justice and is, therefore, no longer outraged by the appearance of "injustice". One concludes, "this is the way the world is and men will take whatever their power enables them to take."

So, too, with Sisyphus the horizon of absent promise has been supplanted with the full presence of the phenomenon of the absurd. "Likewise, the absurd man, when he contemplates his torment, silences all the idols. In the universe suddenly restored to its silence, the myriad wondering little voices of the earth rise up. Unconscious, secret calls, invitations from all the faces, they are the necessary reverse and price of victory. There is no sun without shadow, and it is essential to know the night. The absurd man says yes and his effort will henceforth be unceasing. If there is a personal fate, there is but one which he concludes is inevitable and dispicable. For the rest, he knows himself to be the master of his days. At last, as Sisyphus returns toward his rock, in that slight pivoting he contemplates that series of unrelated actions which becomes his fate, created by him, combined under his memory's eye and soon sealed by his death. Thus, convinced of the wholly human origin of all that is human, a blind man eager to see who knows that the night has no end, he is still on the go. The rock is still rolling."[31]

The inner happiness of Sisyphus, through reversal of all previously beheld aspirations and esteemed values, is won at a great price indeed. He may be henceforth master of his days, but his days are now seen as a night that has no end. The universe may at a stroke be restored to its silence, but it is robbed of its claiming authority along with release from its terror. Its silence is indistinguishable from the nothingness that is prior to creation. As Macbeth would have it, on the point of his suicide, he wishes that it were as black as though the world had never been[32]. Camus rejects personal suicide for the collective ontological negation of being in life. One has purchased an outlook upon a world whose visage is as "inevitable and dispicable" only by closing one's eyes to what one has already seen. It is just as he says, "a blind man eager to see who knows that the night has no end"; yet, unlike Oedipus he has plucked out his eyes before the play even begins.

The direction taken by Camus in the 'Myth of Sisyphus' is already anticipated and countered by Dostoevsky's man from underground who understands more clearly than Camus the wages exacted in the facile reduction of consciousness of the world to a world of consciousness. For the underground man, Camus's statement that "there is no fate that cannot be surmounted by scorn" has a double meaning.

It is exactly the nothingness of the unending night that the scorn of Camus's Sisyphus leaves untouched. For Dostoevsky is aware that in the face of "the things that are not" only 'ressentiment' can make them appear "as the things that are". Dostoevsky rejects Camus's notion that lucidity of one's condition is alone sufficient grounds for authentic tragedy. For the underground man, though fully cognizant of the absurdity of what passes for life above ground, cannot live without aspiring for a life of action and meaning. It is this existential restlessness — the longing for exteriority — that drives him out of his mouse hole to his failed experiments with becoming human above ground.

The underground man shares with the Sisyphus of Camus a revulsion against the limits imposed upon him by the silent universe which appears to him in the guise of the laws of nature. The laws of nature are imaged by him as a stone wall impossible to surmount: "The impossible means the stone wall! What stone wall? Why, of course the laws of nature, the deductions of natural science, mathematics."[33] The unfolding historical consciousness of the natural world, its laws and limits, "the laws of nature and arithmetic" inform the design of the parallel, unfolding social order which has, in advance of his decision, assigned the underground man a fixed place:

"As soon as they prove to you, for instance that you are descended from the monkey, then it is no use scowling, accept it for a fact. When they prove to you that in reality one drop of your own fat must be dearer to you than a hundred thousand of your fellow-creatures, and that this conclusion is the final solution of all so called virtues and duties and all such prejudices and fancies, then you have to accept it, there is no help for it, for twice two is a law of mathematics. Just try refuting it!"[34]

It is owing to the conscious knowledge of such laws that the emerging society of the present is being engineered having "taken your whole register of human advantages from the average of statistical figures and politico-economic formulas".[35] Human advantages are calculated in advance in accordance with the newly discovered laws of "prosperity, wealth, freedom, peace — and so on".[36] Prosperity, for example is guaranteed because science will teach man the laws of economics: "New economic relations will be established, already-made and worked out with mathematical exactitude, so that every possible question will vanish in the twinkling of an eye, simple because every possible answer to it will be provided."[37] The myth of human freedom will be dispelled, and along with it war, when human actions are rendered calculable and inevitable:

"All human actions will then, of course, be tabulated according to these laws, mathematically, like tables of logarithms up to 108,000, and entered in an index; or, better still, there will be published certain well-intentioned works in the nature of encyclopaedic dictionaries in which everything will be so clearly calculated and noted that there will be no more deeds or adventures in the world."[38]

When all human action can be predicted, a substitute will be found for deeds and adventures. Not the inner psychic drama of consciousness coming upon itself, but a Palace of Crystal will be enthroned, designed in accordance with the newly discovered laws of human happiness. Since happiness has at last been unmasked as the absence of unpleasurable sensations, the Crystal Palace will program out everything that is harsh and uncomfortable. Doubt and suffering will disappear along with freedom and self-consciousness. There will be no cause for taking offense in the world of the Crystal Palace because there will be nothing to take offense at. How can one take offense at the laws of nature which, when deciphered, have eliminated the source of all resentment? In the palace of crystal each man becomes transparent to himself and to every other man. Therefore, there can be no quarrels because the screen covering all private motives will have been lifted.

The underground man confesses that, despite all this, even "though the laws of nature have continually and all my life offended me more than anything"[39], the laws of nature cannot be blamed for the self-reproach he feels in the face of his apparently senseless suffering. Against the laws of nature expressed in the image of the Crystal Palace suffering must be invented, contrived, brought about by one's own ungrateful spite. "Simply you will ask why did I worry myself with such antics?"[40] His antics are the vows of reform taken impetuously just after refusing to embrace all that passed as good and beautiful, and doing loathesome things when closest to what was called beautiful and good. The reason for his self-willed suffering begins to emerge when we realize that the underground man will not submit to the reduction of the beautiful to pleasurable sensations and the good to mere utility. Such a reduction may bring an absence of suffering, but it does so at the price of a consciousness that is literally disoriented; that is, going nowhere.

Disoriented consciousness appears in the guise of innocuous boredom. The power of boredom to express a fundamental truth about the nature of the relation between man and his world is not to be underestimated. The underground man supplies a stunning answer to his own question concerning his strange antics.

"Answer: because it was very dull to sit with one's hands folded, and so one began cutting capers. That is really it. Observe yourselves more carefully, gentlemen, then you will understand that it is so. I invented adventures for myself and made up a life so at least to live in some way. How many times it has happened to me — well, for instance, to take offense simply on purpose, for nothing; and one knows oneself, of course, that one is offended at nothing, that one is putting it on but yet one brings oneself, at last to the point of being really offended. All my life I have had an impulse to play such pranks, so that in the end I could not control it in myself."[41]

How can this experiment with self-induced and premeditated delusion be explained?

The experience of boredom implies that one's attention is not commanded by one's surroundings. The immediacy of relation is weakened to the point where one recognizes oneself as outside of, and in that sense detached from, the objects which usually prefigure a hierarchy of attractions and repulsions, priorities and possibilities, interests and obligations. The selectivity of attending to this matter, rather than that, appears now as arbitrary and capricious. One recognizes that in the absence of meaning imprinted in the expressions of the faces or things around one, one must bestow meaning oneself. Therefore, by a fiat of the imagination one etches expressions that appear meaningful in the anonymous, faceless world of men and things, "So one makes up adventures for oneself and a life, so as at least to live in some way," i.e. in a world where one can recognize oneself.

The inner dynamic of boredom is despair. Despair emerges out of boredom when one recognizes the arbitrariness of the self-inventoried fiction one has created. Resentment against consciousness itself, in turn, emerges out of despair when one recognizes that one has fictionalized a drama for oneself as one would spin a world out of one's head, as Zeus contrives Athena out of his brain. Therefore, one does the only thing left. He remains awake. That is to say, he will not let go of his suffering which awakens him to the possibility of standing defiant in the face of the nothingness. Better to take offense on purpose, and for nothing, than to let go of the promise of purpose and take offense against life.

The underground man understands himself as a superfluous, arbitrary creature who has no inherent reason for existing. Yet, he jealously guards his own suffering, for it is his suffering that attunes him to the ground of reality as he comprehends it and which, thereby, offers him at least the illusion of resistance to the forces of somnolence and living death. He will not knowingly deceive himself. Defined by that which he resists and stands against, he cares for nothing. Here is the appearance of the radical inversion and embodiment of the Platonic concept of eros[42]. Deformed eros is known by what it scorns not by what it loves. The underground man pursues the absence of self-deception. This is the single and controlling maxim by which he lives, the one fact that spares his life from scorn. And, it is for this reason that he must summon up the courage to live, somehow, in the absence of self-understanding.

D. The Gesture of Spite: Ressentiment and Recoil

How, then does the underground man resolve his problem? He has recourse to spite as his mode of dealing with the persons and situations he encounters. What is the spite of the underground man? In what way, if at all, is his response to the problem more adequate than Camus's Sisyphus? Kaufmann's opinion is that there is no significant difference. An explanation of the underground man's thought and conduct expressed in the circular relationship of cause and effect, between Parts I and II of the 'Notes' demonstrates the unique function of spitefulness in his war against the Crystal Palace.

It is the theory of Part I which causes the failures in his relationships as manifested in the events of Part II. This can be seen instanced in his grotesquely exaggerated sense of humiliation and his desire for revenge upon the police officer who had roughly hurried him along in the crowd. The underground man invests the meaning of this situation with a sense of injustice.

"This was a regular martyrdom, a continual, intolerable humiliation at the thought, which passed into an incessant and direct sensation, that I was a mere fly in the eyes of all this world, a nasty, disgusting fly — more intelligent, more highly developed, more refined in feeling than any of them, of course — but a fly that was continually making way for everyone, insulted and injured by everyone[43]. 'Why must you invariably be the first to move aside?' I kept asking myself in hysterical rage, waking up sometimes at three o'clock in the morning. 'Why is it you and not he? There's no regulation about it; there's no written law. Let the making way be equal as it usually is when refined people meet'."[44]

To the underground man, it is inconceivable, and hence unjust, that a mere police officer would not bestow the recognition owed to a man of intelligence and refinement. The exaggerated taking of offense finds its expression in a desire for revenge that is even more pronounced. For two years he is consumed by the thought of revenge and is victimized by its bizarre expression: for two years the stealthy enquiries about the officer, the writing of a satirical novel about the incident, going into debt to properly attire himself for the occasion. The fruit of this labor is the temporary expression of pleasure over the comedy of having avenged himself — unbeknownst to the officer — by the "rubbing of shoulders".

Only the concept of the Crystal Palace can explain how such a minor event could be no less significant than a major catastrophe. In a world dominated by the Crystal Palace there can be no difference between justice and revenge. Justice demands the capacity to interpret the surplus suffering caused by the warrantless intention to inflict harm. In the Crystal Palace, however, there is no place for suffering of any kind. This means that there is no way of accounting for the possibility of justice. In the world of the Crystal Palace all suffering must be self-induced. Hence, there is only revenge masking itself as justice. Hence, the paralysis of the will on the part of the man from underground, who wills to suffer, and keeps open the option of protesting the reduction of justice to revenge practiced in the name of the Crystal Palace. Stymied in the world above ground by the objectifying looks of the other, he lives vindictively. In a like manner the man from the underground bemoans the absence of authentic friendship and love, conceptually, only to express the inversion of their respective meanings, existentially.

What the situations with the officer, the underground man's reunion with his childhood friends, and his relation with Lizavetta, the prostitute, have in common is that they are all expressions of spite. What must be shown is how these instances of spite on the part of the underground man are consistent with his conceptual reflection in Part I.

The underground man has chosen to live with suffering, although he is not a masochist. Unlike Sisyphus he refuses to believe that happiness is a state of mind. He insists on retaining the Aristotelian view that happiness is a work (*ergon*), an activity of the soul in accordance with excellence (*arete*). The ultimate, self-defining *arete* of man, the rational animal, *zoon logikon echon*, is reason itself. It is the work of reason that expresses man's ultimate end, the happiness of living fully as the animal endowed with reason (*logos*). The Crystal Palace, however, has enjoined reason to madness by absorbing a life of deeds. It has turned against Aristotle's intention by transforming the meaning of being human, engendering the paradoxical and unacceptable antinomies that force one to choose between freedom and "happiness", thought and action.

The underground man concludes that it would sometimes be better "if two and two did not always equal four". His only refuge is to hole up and hold out in the underground, driven back down by the thought: Better I should go back and nourish myself at the source of my suffering than to give in to the delusion that this is man. Or in his own words: "You say, science itself will teach man ... that he never has really had any caprice or will of his own, and that he himself is something in the nature of a piano key or the stop of an organ ... then the 'Crystal Palace' will be built."[45]

The underground man chooses suffering over what passes for happiness. It is the source towards which he returns in the absence of an authentic expression of happiness. He holds fast to one horn of the impossible dilemma: freedom *or* happiness:
"One's own free unfettered choice, one's own capirce, however wild it may be, one's own fancy worked up at times to frenzy — is that very 'most advantageous advantage' which we have overlooked, which comes under no classification and against which all systems and theories are continually being shattered to atoms."[46]

But, to make such a choice he must struggle against the anaesthetization of the Crystal Palace.

His strategy for staying awake is spite. The mode of its implementation is sabotage. He refuses to consult a doctor "from spite".[47] He explains how he behaved toward petitioners when he worked as an official: "I used to grind my teeth at them, and felt intense enjoyment when I succeeded in making anybody unhappy."[48]

But as the action of Part II reveals, sabotage only brings him heartache which, in turn, intensifies his spite. When Lizavetta, the prostitute, expresses her love for the underground man, he treats her shamelessly and spitefully. He suffers remorse, and reflects on its meaning:

"To fall down before her, to sob with remorse, to kiss her feet, to entreat her forgiveness! I longed for that, my whole breast was being rent to pieces, and never, never shall I recall that minute with indifference. But — what for, I thought. Should I not begin to hate her, perhaps even tomorrow, just because I had kissed her feet."[49]

The underground man is driven to his last refuge, spite against the reader:

"Now, are not you fancying, gentlemen that I am expressing remorse for something now, that I am asking your forgiveness for something? I am sure you are fancying that . . . However, I assure you I do not care if you are."[50]

Ultimately, then, spite is itself exposed by Dostoevsky as a problem for the emblematic man from the underground.

For, as a solution to his dilemma, spite remains on the same level as that of the problem. It cannot escape the tyranny of the Crystal Palace. The Crystal Palace represents time frozen. The underground man must act within time. His sabotage is arrested finally by the residues of remorse that accompany the finality of his temporal acts. He is impotent to direct himself against the freezing of time itself. The self withim time, which understands that temporality itself is the problem, even the enemy, has grasped hold of a profound philosophic dilemma. Yet, in the absence of a new self, prepared for by philosophic reflection, the man from the underground is fated to turn his spite against himself, recreating a life involved in the painful and trivial task of unmaking itself.

The underground man dimly grasps the meaning of his imprisoned self-reflection: "Resentment — why is it purification; it is a most stinging and painful consciousness!" He addresses a question to the reader which he is unable to answer: ". . . I . . . ask on my own account . . . one idle question: which is better — cheap happiness or exalted suffering? Well, which is better?"[51] He has chosen suffering but is not spared the desire to get even for the offenses he has suffered. Fixated in the position of resentment from which the spirit of revenge issues only through half-hearted or symbolic gestures, the man from underground broods incessantly on the objects of his resentment.

The desire for revenge is bottled-up and, in that sense, itself goes underground. Unable to gain revenge, overwhelmed by the tyranny of the Crystal Palace, brooding in his underground lair, the underground man has experienced all of the conditions leading to the structure of what Nietzsche characterized as "Ressentiment":

". . . every sufferer instinctively seeks a cause for his suffering . . . — in short, some living thing upon which he can, on some pretext or other vent his affects, actually or in effigy: for the venting of his affects represents the greatest attempt on the part of the suffering to win relief, *anaesthesia* — the narcotic he cannot help desiring to deaden pain of an kind. This alone constitutes the actual physiological cause of *ressentiment*, vengefulness and the like: a desire to *deaden pain by means of affects.*"[52]

The underground man, however, refuses to be anaesthetized, he insists on staying awake, constantly returning to the source of his suffering, he repeats the endless cycle of self-negating spite. The overcoming of the temporal impasse symbolized by the Crystal Palace is not to be his to perform. It is in this regard that the understanding of Dostoevsky transcends that of his character.

Dostoevsky darkly insinuates in the 'Notes from the Underground' the possible consequences of freedom turned inward against itself in two fundamental elaborations given form in the later novels. In 'The Possessed' freedom is identified as the unbridled expression of the will-to-power, the hyper-conscious mouse has here become the man of action who crushes all stone-walls, reigning in his power of unlimited self-assertion. Nikolai Stavrogin of 'The Possessed' personifies Dostoevsky's anticipation and rejection of the "supra-man". 'Ressentiment' is overcome at the the expense of a world where everything is permitted. 'Ressentiment' against temporality is overcome only by showing itself heedless of the consequences attending the exteriority of the other. Stavrogin, Dostoevsky's experiment with "supra-man", turns his limitless self-assertion against himself and commits suicide out of boredom.

Prefigured in the 'Notes' is Dostoevsky's consummate portrait of 'ressentiment', Ivan Karamazov. He thinks like Raskolnikov, speaks like Stavrogin and acts like an above ground version of the man from the 'Notes'. He embraces the view of freedom understood as the will-to-power, fully aware of its consequences. The 'ressentiment' of Ivan Karamazov is addressed both against a world in which everything is permitted and against his own will which bends back against itself in the face of this knowledge. Smerdyakov acts as the literary as well as the philosophical "double" of Ivan; i.e., he acts out the unconscious revenge born of the 'ressentiment' Ivan harbors within the dark side of his own soul. Ivan plants the seed of the murder of Father Karamazov in the mind of his dull-witted half-brother. Smerdyakov murders Father Karamazov whom Ivan hates passionately. When Ivan discovers that Smerdyakov has murdered his father, he asks with an air of feigned incomprehension why he has done it, to which Smerdyakov truthfully replies: "Don't you know Ivan, I did it for you."[53] Dostoevsky makes unmistakably clear the fact that there is behind the finger of revenge that triggers the murder by Smerdyakov a straight, if invisible line, leading back to the 'ressentiment' buried in the brain of Ivan Karamazov.

To the man from the underground, who harbors the projections of Raskolnikov, Ivan Karamazov, and Stavrogin within his own soul, Dostoevsky withholds all solutions, even the succor of 'ressentiment'. He refuses him friendship and love not because they are false solutions; rather, for a man who lives backwards, 're-sensing' the insult issuing from the faces of contemporary life, such resolutions are partial and premature. Nor, as we have shown, will Dostoevsky permit the man from underground to deny his longing for an authentic life above ground.

Dostoevsky refuses to conclude from his presentation of the life of hyper-self-consciousness either that existence is necessarily absurd or that we must imagine the underground man, as Camus imagines Sisyphus, "happy":

"Now, I am living out my life in my corner taunting myself with the spiteful and *useless* consolation that an intelligent man cannot become anything seriously, and it is only the fool who becomes anything."[54]

The inward apprehension of the absence of an outlook appears in the mirror of the underground as an expressionless face. Spitefulness is for the man from the underground the mask of life, that hides the expression of the death of meaning. In his suffering, in his indecision, he does the only thing he can; he holds out for a more profound diagnosis and the hope of a remedy to the illness he has so acutely experienced, and spoken of to the reader in the first words of his confession. "I am a sick man ... I am a spiteful man ... I believe my liver is diseased."[55]

II. THE PHENOMENOLOGY OF 'RESSENTIMENT': SCHELER

A. Introduction

Transforming the image of 'ressentiment' pictured in the sensory tangle of lived-experience into a phenomenon that can be interpreted by philosophic discourse (*logos*) is a complex and painstaking task. Max Scheler's work 'Ressentiment', published in 1912, is the philosophic work that has undertaken this project. In this chapter of the book we shall take a searching look at Scheler's study.

This brilliant and erratic text offers the natural, and perhaps only logical, point of departure for a radical phenomenological enquiry into the subject of 'ressentiment'. Scheler's work accomplishes two purposes: 1) it provides the framework for discovering, at least in silhouette, the eidetic structure of 'ressentiment'; 2) it offers an amazingly insightful, if in important places defective, description of the factical shape of the patterned structures of 'ressentiment' in the life-world of contemporary existence.

However, in part because of a failure to rigorously execute the phenomenological reduction, Scheler's investigation into 'ressentiment' has concealed the ontological dimension of the phenomenon. The failure to offer an adequate reflection on method, or to practice the *epoche* of the phenomenological reduction, prefigures as well an inadequate solution which Scheler advances to resolve the existential dilemma posed by 'ressentiment'. The enquiry into the phenomenology of 'ressentiment', as presented by Scheler, will be in the spirit of reconstruction and partial rehabilitation. Very few references to Nietzsche will be presented, even though Scheler regarded his own work as carrying to completion the project Nietzsche inaugurated. The necessity for permitting Nietzsche to speak in the first person will emerge as the consequence of our exploration of Scheler.

B. Problem of Method

Scheler distinguishes two methods of investigation which reveal different aspects of the same phenomena. The first method, "influenced by the natural sciences", is essentially concerned with explaining the causal connections which have determined the appearance of the phenomenon. Scheler calls this the "synthetic-constructive" method, and points to it as a prominent approach in contemporary psychology[56].

It follows a procedure comprised of four discernible, sequential steps: 1) The sifting of the data of inner observation; 2) The recognition of the sifted data into compound and conjoined elements; 3) The decomposition of those same compounds into essential constitutive simple elements; 4) The study, through artificial variation, by observation and experimentation, of the results of the simple elements in combinations with each other.

Scheler's characterization of this first "method" suffers from two defects. He makes no attempt to attach the generalized characterization of the four principles mentioned to even a possible inquiry into the subject of 'ressentiment'. Secondly, there is no explicit attempt to distinguish psychological enquiry from philosophical analysis.

Scheler adopts the second approach, which is as much defined by its simple opposition to the "synthetic-constructive" method as it is positively defined by him. This second method Scheler calls "analytic or descriptive psychology"[57]. While the method of "synthetic-constructive" psychology operates with artifically created mental units, descriptive psychology is concerned with the "experience and meaning contained in the totalities of man's life"[58]. The descriptive method is said to focus on the "understandable context" in mental life as opposed to a preoccupation with establishing causal connections[59].

An attempt at the clarification of this distinction refers us to sense-perception. In the case of the "synthetic-constructive" method, mental units derived from sense perception are "artifically created" and, therefore, "I can unite them at will into combinations or analyze such combinations into parts".[60] Scheler cites the case of a diversity of sense perceptions which the mind may simultaneously entertain. The units of experience from which sense perceptions are derived, or which they are intended to represent, are logically distinguishable from the causes or intentions governing the origination or interpretation of the experience. The "synthetic-constructive" method need not pay attention to the content of sense-perceptions in order to determine the chronology of appearances and thus to "interpret" them.

Scheler illustrates this point by briefly describing the objective and subjective aspects of the phenomenon of human equilibrium.

Equilibrium results from the sensations of the inner ear and is control-
led by the functioning of the statolith of the ear[61]. The continuing
sense of equilibrium belongs to a unified, continuous experience
which normally excludes the awareness of the factual presence of the
statolith[62]. The knowledge of the anatomy of the ear does not inform
us as to how we feel balanced or unbalanced or how we are aware of
ourselves as beings who hear in the act of hearing. Questions of anatomy are raised from within the standpoint of experience when a
disruption of equilibrium or hearing takes place. The senses of equilibrium or hearing are associated with non-reducible meanings such as
poise or its absence, and the multiple meanings involved in the act
of listening or the capacity to understand the spoken word. Scheler
suggests that the 'descriptive-analytic' method could be employed
in exploring such phenomena.

The descriptive method assumes the existence of "units of experience and action" which are "phenomenologically simple"[63]. There
are four distinguishable features given by Scheler to characterize
phenomenologically simple units of experience and action. First,
these data possess contents that are multifaceted, heterogeneous,
and perspectival. Such contents will include "sensations, represen-
tations, conclusions, judgments, acts of love, hatred, feelings, moods,
etc."[64]. The examples given by Scheler are followed by others, without explanation or regard to the apparent incommensurability of
epistemological status: an experience of friendship, or love, an insult,
and "an overall attitude toward my environment in a phase of childhood"[65].

Scheler is struggling to show that there are "subjective" phenomena that must be capable of objectification and, hence, descriptive
analysis if the lived-world of everyday existence is to be made accessible to thought. However, Scheler's failure to distinguish in a clear
manner the activity of thought from the objects of thought prefigures
an essential confusion in his investigation of 'ressentiment'. In our
reconstruction of Scheler we shall emphasize the noetic and noematic
aspects of the formal structure of 'ressentiment', which Scheler, at
times, runs together.

As the second criterion for distinguishing the "phenomenologically simple units of experience and action" Scheler calls attention to
the fact that such units are discontinuous with objectively conceived
time, suffering as they do from diurnal interruptions and transitions.
Given Scheler's preliminary emphasis on the aspects of 'ressentiment'

associated with the "repeated experiencing and re-living" of the phenomenon, we should expect some methodological clarification on the relation of lived-time to objectively conceived time. To broach the meaning of 'ressentiment' necessitates an analysis of its temporal character. Scheler's methodological failure here prefigures a concealing of the ontological dimension of the phenomenon. We shall see how the suppression of the ontological dimension in Scheler's treatment of the problem of 'ressentiment' affects both his exploration of the phenomenon and his attempt to provide an adequate solution to the existential questions raised by its presentation.

The third and fourth criteria intended to distinguish phenomenologically simple units of experience and action are stated, but not analyzed, by Scheler: 3) These "units of experience ... I feel to be active", though "not as objective causes", but rather in the sense of being "instrumental in determining my actions"[66]. 4) "These partial units must always receive their meaning and unity through *one* act of experience, not through an artificial separation and synthesis."[67] Scheler does not further clarify either the *intentional* character of such action, or what is signified by the *unitary* nature of such experience (*Erfahrung*). The concept of experience and the problem of the constitution of meaning remain unprobed. Scheler's reflections on method are important because the questions which here remain unasked exercise a subtle, but pervasive control over his enquiry into 'ressentiment'. The failure to acknowledge the phenomenological reduction is evidenced in the fact that an *epoche* is not practiced upon the "natural attitude".

Scheler may not have told us how to recognize a "unit of experience", but he is sure about his own objective. The primary task which he sets himself is to "penetrate more deeply into the *unit of experience* designated by the term (*ressentiment*)"[68]. Notice, however, the revealing discourse that Scheler employs in his provisional characterization of the phenomenon:

"Ressentiment is a self-poisoning of the mind which has quite definite causes and consequences. It is a lasting mental attitude, caused by the systematic repression of certain emotions and affects which, as such, are normal components of human nature. Their repression leads to the constant tendency to indulge in certain kinds of value delusions and corresponding value judgments. The emotions and affects primarily concerned are revenge, hatred, malice, envy, the impulse to detract, and spite."[69]

From a phenomenological point of view, the discourse Scheler employs to speak about 'ressentiment' is striking in the absence of attention to the assumptions sedimented in crucial word-concepts that govern his description. Scheler is content to identify 'ressentiment' as an "emotion" without probing the general bias against "emotion" as a mode of cognition.

The assumption which positions 'ressentiment' into a chain of "causes" and "effects" without calling attention to its "phenomenologically simple" character is noteworthy. From a phenomenological standpoint, this philosophically uncritical language introducing the phenomenon of 'ressentiment' serves, against Scheler's intention, to suggest that he is proposing a genetic, psychological account of a subjective emotion.

Scheler's assurance that such emotions and affects "are normal components of human nature" does not inform us as to what Scheler takes "human nature" to mean, and in no place in the text is this question raised. Language about "mental attitudes", "value judgments", and the mention of "repression" add to the impression that Scheler's subsequent analysis fits within the previously disparaged "synthetic-constructivistic" approach. The failure to perform the phenomenological reduction is responsible for Scheler's refusal to bracket a Cartesian matrix of assumptions: that the subject is isolated from the world; that mind is independent of body; that the passions, however important, are not significant in constituting the meaning of objectivity; that judgments of value belong to a separate and presumably unrelated sphere from judgments of fact.

Given all of these reservations concerning the absence of careful methodological consideration on Scheler's part, it is still meaningful to use the word "phenomenological" to characterize the nature of his approach in a general way. For Scheler is concerned to describe the phenomenon of 'ressentiment' as it makes its appearance within the general context of what Husserl calls the *Lebenswelt*. He is concerned with investigating the phenomenon as it "looks" to man prior to any conceptual interpretation of its epistemological or metaphysical implications; that is, within the originary context of the swirl of his everyday concerns. In that respect, the demand to weigh the truth or falsity of Scheler's assertions concerning the nature of 'ressentiment' must be posterior to the phenomenologically prior question of the first objectification of the phenomenon as an appearance possessed of cognitive status because of the meaningful character it expresses in the context of the life-world.

Critics of Scheler should keep in mind that phenomenology is often so preoccupied with problems of method that the prescription of Husserl's maxim, "to the things themselves", is set aside in favor of endlessly searching for the path to be followed to the things themselves. Scheler here is a notable exception. He is like an explorer who proceeds without a detailed map, knowing generally where he wants to go, but who is relatively indifferent to the hazards in his way or unconcerned to explain to future travelers how to follow his own journey. Or, perhaps he is like St. Exupery's drunken map-maker who imperils all would-be explorers. Still, Scheler has left a detailed and searching journal of events that have befallen him on his way, and it is to this carefully kept log that we shall now turn our attention.

C. The Hermeneutics of 'Ressentiment'

Scheler offers general criteria for determining the actual appearance of the phenomenon of 'ressentiment'. The single and most important source of the phenomenon which Scheler points to is the desire for revenge (*Rache*). 'Ressentiment' appears when the thirst for revenge cannot be slaked. Revenge that leads to 'ressentiment' commences when, and only when: 1) the subject experiences an attack or injury occasioned at the hands of another; 2) there exists a component of delay or procrastination that intensifies both the experience of hurt and the anger to redress the original injury; 3) impotence on the part of the injured subject is responsible for occasioning delay; 4) it is "of the essence of revenge that it always contains the consciousness of 'tit for tat'."[70] Scheler concludes without explanation that because it is of the essence of revenge to possess consciousness of the desire for equity in retribution, "it is never a *mere* emotional reaction."[71]

Scheler specifies further the necessity to distinguish the desire for revenge, which he classifies as a "reactive impulse", from all "active and aggressive impulses"[72]. He cites two counter-examples to illustrate the proper language used to describe revenge. He says that it is incorrect to speak of revenge when an animal bites its attacker[73]. Presumably, this is because criterion 3) above (consciousness) is lacking. The second counter-example is reprisal immediately following a box on the ear[74]. It is significant that Scheler does not dwell on how the phenomenon of delay can or does manifest itself, either in general or in the examples cited.

Scheler proceeds with a description of the "genealogy" born of revenge leading to 'ressentiment' proper. He speaks of a "progression of feeling" beginning with revenge, moving to rancor, envy, and the impulse to detract, and then developing into spite. Scheler catalogues the above emotions, presenting a detailed topology of their delimited characters, but without specifying the kind of noetic activity corresponding to the "progression of feeling" leading to 'ressentiment'[75].

According to Scheler, revenge and envy possess a structural similarity in that each possesses a specific intentional object. The object governing the genesis of revenge and envy need not be specific. It is, in fact, important to note that, for Scheler, forgetfulness of the original object engendering revenge or envy serves as an indispensable precondition for the eventual emergence of 'ressentiment'.

The impulse to detract (*Scheelsucht*) is distinguishable from revenge and envy in that it is not possessed by an intentional object. The impulse to detract possesses three distinguishable and interrelated aspects. In the first place, it will not submit to a genealogical account just because it does not appear and disappear with the advent of specific causes and consequences. Therefore, it is logically inconceivable that it have a history, such as revenge or envy. Secondly, the very expression of the impulse to detract attains its satisfaction coincident with its expression. Prior to any given situation in which concrete envy manifests itself, the impulse to detract is always on the lookout to 'disparage' the appearance of any expression of excellence. The impulse to detract surges forward, prepared to break images and smash idols from their pedestals[76]. In maintaining that the impulse to detract "fashions each concrete experience of life and selects it from possible experience"[77], Scheler suggests a significant phenomenological distinction. In maintaining in this connection that "there is set a fixed pattern of experience which can accommodate the most diverse contents"[78], Scheler can be seen to be groping his way towards a conception of the *a priori* that is material. The confusion surrounding the ontological status of Scheler's "genealogical" investigation can be traced in the main to the fact that in this, his first book, the concept of a material *a priori* has not yet attained conceptual clarity[79].

Spite (*Hämischkeit*) is presented by Scheler as the radicalization of the impulse to detract, where the latter is always close to the surface and "ready to burst forth and to betray itself in an unbridled gesture, a way of smiling, etc."[80]. It is unclear whether Scheler means to say that spite reveals the impulse to detract as the latter has become second nature, or whether the impulse to detract can be known only through the manifestations of a spiteful countenance. Scheler remarks that "an analogous road leads from simple *Schadenfreude* (joy at another's misfortune) to 'malice' "[81]. In a manner that is at once suggestive and ambiguous, he states: "The latter (malice-*Bosheit*), more detached than the former (*Schadenfreude*) from definite objects, tries to bring about ever new opportunities for *Schadenfreude*."[82] In what sense, we may ask, is malice prior to joy at the misfortune of another? Certainly, malice may manifest itself in an active and self-conscious intention to do the other injury or harm. As presented by Scheler, it is valid to infer that the reaction to the misfortune of another depends upon a prior disposition or intention towards the other in his generality, and which, in turn, serves to inform the content of the given reaction.

The "progression of feeling"[83] and the "stages in the development of its (i.e.) 'ressentiment's') sources"[84] as presented by Scheler may be summarized as follows;

1) Revenge (*Rache*)   → Rancor (*Groll*)   → Impulse to
                                            Detract
                                            (*Scheelsucht*)

Definite Object	Status of Object Unclear	Absence of a Definite Object

Spite (*Hämischkeit*)

Definite Object

                              and

2) Impulse to Detract   Malice (absence of a Definite Object)
   ──────────────────   ─────────────────────────────────────
   Spite   *Schadenfreude* (Definite Object)

Scheler has introduced his reflection on the stages of the development of 'ressentiment' by calling attention to the noematic objects through which 'ressentiment' is revealed. Scheler is, however, equivocal as to how the stages in the sources of 'ressentiment' yield 'ressentiment' as such. He says only "Yet, all this is not *ressentiment*."[85]

It remains completely ambiguous whether any or all of the stages existentially co-implicate the others. Are the stages, characterized as sources of 'ressentiment', possessed of an existential sequentiality in relation to one another, or are their appearances simultaneous? Again, Scheler has submerged the temporal dimension of the phenomenon.

What then is 'ressentiment' as such according to Scheler? Rather than answering the question directly, Scheler describes those conditions under which 'ressentiment' can and does appear and those conditions which specifically legislate the absence of its appearance. Scheler limits this discussion to 'ressentiment' which has its source in the desire for revenge.

'Ressentiment' as such cannot appear in the presence of acts of "moral self-conquest". Forgiveness is mentioned as an act of this kind. Scheler does not say what genuine forgiveness is, or whether forgiveness might cause 'ressentiment' to disappear once it has appeared. Secondly, a direct expression of vengeance against the agent held responsible for occasioning insult or injury will obviate the possible appearance of 'ressentiment'. Third, even the gesture of anger betokening intended revenge will be sufficient to preclude the possible appearance of 'ressentiment'. This third negative condition must, however, be accompanied by "a pronounced awareness of impotence"[86] on the part of the subject. Scheler maintains a fourth negative condition stipulating that even speech in the presence of a third person expressing a desire on the part of the subject to gain vengeance, even when impotence renders this impossible, will be sufficient to prevent the appearance of 'ressentiment'. All of these four conditions legislate the absence of 'ressentiment' because the desire for revenge is either expressed in one way, or in the case of "acts of moral self-conquest", the desire is genuinely overcome.

There are several positive conditions which must prevail, according to Scheler, if 'ressentiment' as such is to appear. Powerful manifestations of the desire for revenge must first be called back from their natural tendency towards expression. The suppressed desire for revenge changes into "actual vindictiveness, the more their direction shifts toward indeterminate groups of objects which need only share one common characteristic, and the less they are satisfied by vengeance taken on a specific object".[87] The movement of suppressed revenge which turns into actual vindictiveness is significant because, in the absence of satisfaction, the paralyzed impulse to take revenge turns diffusely against a class of objects that is held to be collectively responsible for inflicting unwarranted injury.

This absence of satisfaction in the face of desired revenge is a second distinguishable criterion, offered by Scheler, which must manifest itself for 'ressentiment' as such to occur. The prolonged experience of the absence of satisfaction, which, in the case of "actual vindictiveness", is derived from the class of objects held responsible for unwarranted suffering, may develop into a profound feeling that one has been singled out for attack because of one's own righteousness.

Scheler does not claim that experiencing an attack or injury as directed against one's own righteousness is a necessary condition for the appearance of 'ressentiment' as such. Such a manifestation of the feeling of righteousness is, however, an extreme expression of vindictiveness. Vindictiveness of this sort becomes apparent when the most innocent actions and innocuous remarks are apprehended with injurious intent, "instinctively and without conscious volition"[88]. The vindictive person is constantly on the lookout for such objects as are capable of satisfying his confirmation of his own sense of rightness. As Scheler says: "Great touchiness is indeed frequently a symptom of vengeful character."[89] 'Ressentiment' as such emerges when the phenomenon of vindictiveness is itself repressed.

However, the very appearance of 'ressentiment' as such is said to require at least two modifications of the suppression of vindictiveness. The repression of the imagination of revenge is expressive of the intensification of the vindictiveness leading to 'ressentiment'. The absence of the image of vengeance leads in turn to a concealing of the emotion in vindictiveness, still acquainted with the original intention to seek revenge.

Through this intricate series of phenomena, in turn revealing and concealing their appearances, 'ressentiment' at last fully manifests itself as a "state of mind"[90]. Scheler's summary statement on the process reads as follows: "Only then does this *state of mind* become associated with the tendency to detract from the other person's value, which brings an illusory easing of the tension."[91]

Although Scheler fails to distinguish between *noesis* and *noemata* in his genealogical account of the appearance of 'ressentiment', the results of Scheler's preceding analysis constitute his clearest statement on the noetic activity of 'ressentiment'-consciousness. Those results may be summarized as follows: 1) Intention to seek revenge → 2) Repression of 1) → 3) Vindictiveness → 4a) Imagination of 3) suppressed 1) intention to seek revenge → 4b) Emotion of 3) suppressed → 5). The complete concealing of 1) and the emergence of 'ressentiment' as a state of mind, with the generalized intention to detract from the value of the other.

Thus Scheler prematurely breaks off his richly suggestive attempt to characterize the phenomenon of 'ressentiment' as such. The remainder of his first work is concerned with applying the original treatment of 'ressentiment' to the varied phenomena of contemporary existence.

Scheler's interpretation of the formal structure of 'ressentiment' raises questions that warrant answers. The questions of the meaning and being of 'ressentiment' remain veiled. What does it mean to say that *"ressentiment* [is] a state of mind . . . associated with the tendency to detract from the other person's value, which brings an illusory easing of the tensions"?[92] What is the injury that sets 'ressentiment' in motion? Does it have a single source with multiple expressions? Is the agent always, or necessarily, perceived as another person or class of persons? Is the subject of 'ressentiment' always, or necessarily, an individual or group of persons, or is being human, always or sometimes, fated to 'ressentiment'? What principles of interpretation govern the designation of 'ressentiment' as a *state of mind . . . associated with the tendency to devalue*?

The force of these relevant philosophic questions need not obscure the positive thrust of Scheler's investigation. We may profitably and provisionally lay aside such questions if a schema can be worked out in which the noetic and noematic aspects of 'ressentiment' can be subtended by an hermeneutical framework that phenomenologically brackets the factual appearances of the phenomenon. As Heidegger remarks concerning the function of an hermeneutical investigation: "The phenomenology of *Dasein* (being there) is a hermeneutic in the primordial signification of this word, where it designates this business of interpreting . . . we may exhibit the horizon of any further ontological study of those entities which do not have the character of *Dasein* . . . this hermeneutic also becomes a 'hermeneutic' in the sense of working out those conditions on which the possibility of any ontological investigation depends."[93]

Given what Scheler has already said, the following structure would remain constant, in advance of any given set of shifting, experiential circumstances, or qualifying characteristics pertaining to a given knowing subject:

Hermeneutical Circle of Ressentiment

Injury
(experienced as wantonly inflicted)

    1) *Suffering*
        (sadness, sorrow)

7) *Denial of Injury*

Calm   2) *Anger*
(Devaluation
of suffering)

    6) *Ressentiment*   3) *Resentment*
       a) Denial of desire
          for revenge
       b) Denial of resentment
       c) Denial of anger   4) *Desire for Revenge*

       5) *Rancor*
         (desire for revenge
         blocked, postponed,
         and/or sublimated)

The existential logic of what we may call the Hermeneutical Circle of 'Ressentiment' has a forward motion that is initiated by 1) *suffering* that is believed by the victim to be inflicted wantonly by an agent held responsible for the suffering occasioned; 2) *anger* is occasioned when the victim recognizes that the suffering generated by the original injury is intentional, unjust, and meant to hurt the victim; 3) in the absence of the expression of righteous indignation *resentment* emerges as the anger informs the content of suffering and adopts an integrated stance towards it (i.e., the combination of suffering and anger); 4) the bottling up of the expression of resentment and the intensification of its desire to express itself governs the appearance of the *desire for revenge*. The intensification of the desire for revenge and the concealment of its expression is transformed into 5) *rancor* when sustained over time; 6) *ressentiment as such* emerges as a strategy for assuaging the original hurt experienced by the injury inflicted, moving backwards and engaging in the progressive denial of 6a the desire for revenge, 6b) resentment, and 6c) anger leading finally to calm, a deval-uation of the source of suffering, and the original injury that sets in motion the circle of 'ressentiment'.

Within the context of Scheler's analysis it remains incomprehen-sible how the set of interlocking *e-motions* move out of one another towards a completion of the meaning of the whole. The hermeneutical circle of 'ressentiment' addresses itself to the existential analytic of *Dasein* such that the actual appearance of any one of the arcs of the circle can be grounded in the horizon of the whole that legislates its possibility. As Heidegger says:

"And finally, to the extent that *Dasein*, as an entity with the possi-bility of existence, has ontological priority over every other entity, 'hermeneutic', as an interpretation of *Dasein*'s Being, has the third and specific sense of an analytic of the existentiality of existence; and this is the sense which is philosophically *primary*."[94]

Let us leave in phenomenological brackets for the time being the question of what constitutes, for Scheler, the primary injury that sets in motion the hermeneutical circle of 'ressentiment'. Furthermore, let us suspend such questions as can be raised concerning the phen-omenologically simple character of such data as suffering, i.e., the relationship of suffering to pain[95]. From a strictly hermeneutical standpoint, we may ask how and why human suffering, and its multi-ple modes of expression, should give rise to the phenomenon of anger? Certainly, there are expressions of human suffering that do not engender the appearance of anger. The purposeful arousal of sadness in a tragic play or melancholic song may be cited as cases where sor-rowing has a cathartic effect, that is deemed to be a good in its own right.

Can "anger as such", however, be said to manifest itself without the prior appearance of suffering? We may wish to say that the phen-omenon of "righteous indignation" proves that anger need not be prepared for by expressions of sadness or sorrow. For when we be-come righteously indignant over the unwarranted good fortune of another, or an unwarranted injury inflicted upon someone else by a third party, we are, as Aristotle maintains in his 'Rhetoric', engaged in authentic expressions of anger where we ourselves have no reason to suffer, as we have not personally been visited with harm. What remains unprobed by Scheler, and unclear on Aristotle's account, is how righteous indignation can manifest itself in the first place[96].

For, if it is the case that anger first appears, and only after the

purification of reflection looks for justification of its own self-expression, then the original injury perceived cannot, in the act of perception, offer to consciousness the possibility of explaining the content of the offense. The wrath of Achilles, for example, is informed
by the grief he experiences over the death of Patroclus[97]; the spitefulness of Dostoevsky's man from the underground makes no sense without the existentially prior appearance of his senseless suffering. Anger
cannot be born of dispassionate solicitude. The material upon which
the anger of righteous indignation works is that of sadness, whether
of the other or myself.

Anger that moves forward toward *resentment* must originate with
the primordial forward motion of sadness. The anger of *resentment*, in
turn, recognizes itself as justified in the face of gratuitious harm
wrought from without. *Resentment*, then, itself moves forward towards the desire for revenge which is the inescapable horizon that
makes its existence philosophically comprehensible. With the expression of the desire for revenge, the circle of 'ressentiment' may be
broken, as Scheler correctly maintains. However, with the concealing
of the desire for revenge and the origination of rancor, the circle invariably recommences, magnified and intensified, fated to 'ressentiment'.

D. The Ontic Appearance of the Phenomenon

The removal of the phenomenological brackets from the hermeneutical circle of 'ressentiment' enables us to ask a fundamental question:
what, for Scheler, is the primary injury that sets the circle of "ressentiment' in motion? What is the nature of the suffering that gives
birth to the anger that leads to resentment, and who or what is responsible for it?

It is the phenomenon Scheler calls 'ressentiment-envy' that is
responsible for setting in motion the wheel of 'ressentiment' as it
spins through the avenues of modern social and political life[98]. The
factual appearance of "ressentiment-envy" is governed by very precise
conditions. Scheler differentiates strata of envy in order to clarify the
conditions under which such radical envy triggers 'ressentiment'[99].

All expressions of envy, according to Scheler are oriented towards
an object that is at once coveted and, because of impotence on the
part of the one who envies, is experienced as out of reach[100]. "Simple

envy" vanishes when the object coveted is possessed. Scheler points to crime, violence, work, and barter as vehicles through which envy may be satisfied and the appearance of 'ressentiment' pre-empted[101].

The feeling of impotence, even when compounded out of the tension between desire and non-fulfillment is insufficient to account for the appearance of "true envy". The latter appears only when, according to Scheler, the owner of the coveted possession is construed as the cause, rather than accidental occasion, of envy[102]. In the mind of the envious person, a hatred of the owner of the coveted object overtakes him and outruns the desire for the object. A delusional interpretation results. The actions of the one possessing the envied object are construed as intentionally directed against the desire of the one who envies.

This falsified consciousness, however, yields a remedial benefit. It reduces the tension between the desire provoking envy and the absence of capacity to satisfy that desire. It does so by presenting the one who envies with a dramatic obstacle that need not reflect an impoverishment of his own sense of self or an awareness of himself as covetous. Even when there exists both a sense of impotence and a delusional confusion regarding efficient cause and accidental occasion, a third condition must be established before the linkage between envy and 'ressentiment' can emerge.

"Ressentiment-envy" manifests itself when coveted goods cannot, because of controlling conditions, be attained. When the illusion prevails that such coveted goods are within the reach of individuals or groups, when in *fact*, they are not, the original suffering occasioned by "simple envy" moves within the horizon of 'ressentiment'.

Scheler deduces the sociological law of 'ressentiment' from the phenomenology of 'ressentiment-envy":
"There follows the important sociological law that this psychological dynamite will spread with the *discrepancy* between the political, constitutional, or traditional status of a group and its *factual* power. It is the difference between these two factors which is decisive, not one of them alone."[103]

Using this sociological law as a springboard, Scheler dives to the depths of the contemporary life-world, exploring the variegated, concrete appearances of 'ressentiment'.

These are recurring situations which, independent of individual temperament are, according to Scheler, "charged with the danger of 'ressentiment' "[104]. Women in general, and the "old maid" in particular, are portrayed by Scheler as cast into situations conducive to the appearance of 'ressentiment'. So, too, are priests in general, and apostates in particular. Criminals in general are exempted because they are usually "active type(s) ... who instead of repressing hatred, revenge, envy and greed ... release them in crime".[105] The exceptions are those criminals for whom there is no practical advantage, when spite, alone, governs the deed; "the arsonist is the purest type"[106].

Why woman in general? Scheler explains:

"She is the weaker and therefore the more vindictive sex. Besides, she is always forced to compete for man's favor, and this competition centers precisely on her personal and unchangeable qualitites. . . The strong feminine tendency to indulge in detractive gossip is further evidence; it is a form of self-cure. The danger of feminine *ressentiment* is extraordinarily intensified because both nature and custom impose upon woman a reactive and passive role in love, the domain of her most vital interest."[107]

Why the "old maid" in particular? Scheler:

". . . the 'old maid' with her repressed cravings for tenderness, sex, and propogation, is rarely quite free of *ressentiment* . . . The habitual behavior of many old maids, who obsessively ferret out all sexually significant events in their surroundings in order to condemn them harshly, is nothing but sexual gratification transformed into *ressentiment* satisfaction. Thus the criticism *accomplishes* the very thing it pretends to condemn."[108]

Note that Scheler is not speaking here of mere 'rationalization', the conversion of a necessity into a virtue, or psychological sublimation, whereby the coveted object is replaced and subsumed on another plane. The reach of 'ressentiment', here secures the original object valued, through the transvaluation of its meaning.

Why the priest in general? Scheler asserts that by virtue of his profession the priest is more exposed to the danger of 'ressentiment' than any other human types, apart from qualifying considerations of temperament and nationality:

". . . he is not supported by secular power, indeed he affirms the fundamental weakness of such power . . . More than any other man, he is condemned to conceal his emotions (revenge, wrath, hatred) at least outwardly, for he must always represent the image and principle of 'peacefulness'. The typical 'priestly policy' of gaining victories through the counterforces which the sight of the priest's suffering produces in men who believe that he unites them with God, is inspired by ressentiment."[109]

Scheler, though inspired here by Nietzsche's description of the priestly function, is, as we shall see, determined to preserve the sanctuary of *homo religiosus* from 'ressentiment'. It should be noted here, however, that Nietzsche was addressing himself primarily to the way by which the priestly type used 'ressentiment' to ascend the rungs on the ladder of temporal power, and once at the top, to remain there[110].

The apostate, almost by definition, is condemned to 'ressentiment'. He is distinguished from the genuine convert to a new religious faith because he defines himself primarily by engaging, as Scheler says, "in a continuous chain of acts of revenge against his own spiritual past . . . and the new faith is merely a handy frame of reference for negating and rejecting the old"[111]. Following Nietzsche, Scheler cites the case of the Roman apostate, Tertullian, who asserted that "the sight of Roman governors burning in hell is one of the chief sources of heavenly beatitude"[112]. It is not by accident, as Scheler notes, again following Nietzsche, that Tertullian, the apostate, should have exclaimed: ". . . *credible est, quia ineptum est, artum est, quia impossible est — credo, quia absurdum.*" Tertullian's "I believe . . . because it is absurd", is, according to Scheler, justifying his new faith in a "continuous vengeance taken on the values of antiquity"[113].

Many other spokes in the wheel of 'ressentiment' are exposed by Scheler, most often without in-depth exploration: The "mother-in-law"[114], especially the mother of the son; "younger children's relation with the first-born son"[115]; "the older wife's with the younger husband"[116]; "retired officials"[117] (Dostoevsky's underground man), prostitutes[118], opposition-out-of-power political groups[119], relations of the generations[120] are all offered as likely candidates for 'ressentiment'.

Scheler singles out the style of modern philosophy in general as expressing 'ressentiment'. He points to its preference for criticism, and the regressive search for a "criterion" to take the measure of errors, a quest which it considers more important to its work than the search for truth. It is obsessed with critiquing the opinions of others and looks with disdain upon understanding "arrived at by direct contact with the world and the objects themselves"[121]. Reflecting a much deeper criticism of Nietzsche's, as we shall see, Scheler ridicules the objective of " 'dialectical method' which wants to produce not only *non*-A, but even B through the negation of A"[122].

The relations between the generations are also marred by the recurring disposition to 'ressentiment' upon the part of older to younger, the previous generation to the one emerging. Perceptively, Scheler states that the phenomenon of aging can be free of 'ressentiment' only by "free *resignation* ... [and] renunciation of the values proper to the preceding stage of life"[123]. If this does not happen, we shall have "envy for the young to whom they [such values] are still accessible"[124].

Scheler's failure to dwell with the phenomenon conceals the ontological dimension of *becoming* old. It is not simply the anxiety over death that is masked. Scheler provocatively cites the observation that "Only when the individual cut himself loose from the community which outlasted him, did the duration of his personal life become his standard of happiness"[125]. What is concealed, on Scheler's account, is that aspect of the phenomenon which informs the structure of temporal unfolding, the urgency which dictates the experienced hierarchy of what is valuable, whether of the person or communities or a generation. How do persons or community or generations *face* 'futures' and 'pasts' which they recognize as belonging to other persons or to themselves? What does it mean to live *my* future from day to day such that it imperceptibly escapes the grasp of others? How can I freely *resign* myself, as Scheler recommends, to the passing of a stage of life if I am unable to answer these questions. It is at this moment that the failure of method shows itself most dramatically. Scheler simply cannot show how *existence* is a phenomenon.

The examples Scheler picks to illustrate his point, in fact, turn against his expressed intention. "Cases of existential envy ... are *rare*"[126], according to Scheler. Such cases are said to be rare because they belong to the lives of great men. But the *existence* of human beings is not rare.

Caesar is singled out as a paradigm case of existential envy[127]. If Caesar is envied by Brutus, because the latter can never *be* Caesar, as Scheler implies, then should one not expect of Scheler a reflection on what it means to *be* Caesar, such that the very perception of his *existence* could serve as the occasion for "the strongest source of *ressentiment*"? Moreover, we should expect to find out how the phenomenon of existential envy serves an analogous function in the formation of 'ressentiment' in everyday life. Scheler, here, recoils from such questioning and, in what is in fact said, serves to veil the phenomenon.

Scheler's complete remarks on the subject of existential envy are as follows:

"In the lives of great men there are always critical periods of instability, in which they alternately envy and try to love those whose merits they cannot but esteem. Only gradually, one of these attitudes will predominate. Here lies the meaning of Goethe's reflection that 'against another's great merits, there is no remedy but love'. In his *Torquato Tasso* (Act II, Scene 3) he suggests that Antonio's relations with Tasso are characterized by this kind of ambiguity. An analagous dynamic situation is seen between Marius and Sulla, Caesar and Brutus. Besides these cases of existential envy, which are rare, the innate characteristics of groups of individuals (beauty, racial excellence, hereditary character traits) are the chief causes of *ressentiment* envy."[128]

The statements "Caesar exists" and "Brutus envies Caesar" must, from Scheler's description above, be susceptible to the following reduction:
1) Caesar is *great*.
2) Brutus is *not* as great as Caesar.
3) Therefore, Brutus envies the *greatness* of Caesar.

The original statement "Caesar exists" tells us nothing, for Scheler, except perhaps to distinguish that Caesar is "living" and, therefore, not dead. In keeping with the general bias of modern philosophy, originating with Kant's refutation, Scheler is committed to the position that *existence* cannot serve as a meaningful *predicate*. Scheler's thought, by moving within the horizon of this assumption, can tell us what Caesar signifies to Brutus only by concealing the question of *who* Brutus *is*, such that he should envy greatness, and who Caesar is, such that greatness should define his *existence*.

We should have to know what Brutus longed to become in order to fully appreciate how and why Caesar was perceived by him as the obstacle to his longing. When was it determined by him that he wanted to *become* Caesar and when was it determined by him that he could not — not in childhood or senescence, before he made Caesar's acquaintance, or when it could no longer make a difference?

Existential envy can manifest itself only in relation to that kind of comparison in which I stand in an envious relation to the finitude of the other. Ontically, such existential envy would show itself in relation to the phenomenon of aging, as Scheler himself has already suggested. Two subjects, "B" and "C", might perceive themselves as superior or inferior to each other in all social, physical, economic, and spiritual respects, and yet "B" would be meaningfully interpreted as manifesting 'ressentiment' against the existence of "C" when "B" recognizes that he can no longer become "C". The other person's sheer existence can serve as an affront, and as a reminder, if, and only if, I can insert myself into a framework of a shared temporality in which I can experience my own being as having been, in some sense, however culturally defined, outstripped by him. Because Scheler does not describe how I *become* the being I *am*, he cannot explain the sheer existence of anyone, and therefore he cannot account for the possibility of any person's envying the *existence* of any other person.

Scheler does more than merely mask the ontological dimension of existential envy. The concept as expressed by him has alarming ethical implications as well. It is perfectly reasonable for Scheler to stress that: "the more the injury is experienced as a destiny . . . a person or group feels that the very fact and quality of its *existence* is matter that calls for revenge."[129] However, when Scheler designates "beauty", "racial excellence", and "hereditary character traits" as the chief causes of "ressentiment-envy" without offering a reflection on how, and by whom, such "immediately" superior characteristics are reckoned, he readies the concept of 'ressentiment' for service in the most reactionary and racist of political regimes. Scheler uncritically and categorically bundles together "cripples . . . people of subnormal intelligence . . . Jewish 'ressentiment' . . . the extremely powerful acquisitive instinct of this people is due to a deep-rooted disturbance of Jewish self-confidence . . . the labor Movement, the conviction that the very existence and fate of the proletariat 'cries for revenge' "[130].

At the hub of the wheel of 'ressentiment' Scheler has refused to distinguish suffering that holds out in the absence of justice, where injustice is the cause of such suffering, from suffering that nourishes itself from the wellsprings of 'ressentiment'. The enquiry into 'ressentiment', here, deviates disappointingly from true philosophical rigor. Otherwise, we should be forced to conclude that the aspiration that holds in the face of absent justice is always an expression of 'ressentiment'. Dostoevsky has already explained the existential consequences that issue from such a reduction.

This turn in Scheler's thought is particularly lamentable just because the concept of 'ressentiment' could be put in the service of liberation rather than oppression. The structure of entire political orders, Scheler profoundly points out, can prefigure the likely emergence of 'ressentiment'. The same axiom that governs the engendering of social types applies, for Scheler, in the case of political systems. From a purely descriptive standpoint, he maintains that political 'ressentiment' is not necessarily a function of economic class or the system of governing, autocratic or democratic. It is again a function of the discrepancy between social status and factual political power. Scheler states:

"Social *ressentiment*, at least, would be slight in a democracy which is not only political, but also social and tends toward equality of property. But the same would be the case — and *was* the case — in a caste society such as that of India, or in a society with sharply divided classes. *Ressentiment* must therefore be strongest in a society like ours, where approximately equal rights (political and otherwise) or formal social equality, publicly recognized, go hand in hand with wide factual differences in power, property, and education. While each has the right to compare himself with everyone else, he cannot do so in fact."[131]

Writing in pre-World War I Germany, Scheler's remarks have an almost prophetic ring to them, especially when read together with the following passage found in another context:

"In present-day society, *ressentiment* is by no means most active in the industrial proletariat (except when it is infected by the *ressentiment* of certain leader types), but rather in the disappearing class of artisans, in the petty bourgeoisie and among small officials. The exact causes of this phenomenon cannot be examined here."[132]

Given what Scheler has said before, it remains unclear where his sympathies would have been.

A just political order would aspire to transform the economic and social structures that inspire 'ressentiment', alleviating the source of unjust suffering. The eradication of political 'ressentiment' cannot be purchased at the price of preventing righteous indignation that gives birth to the pursuit of justice. Nor can the task of philosophy rest content to anaesthetize man to the ascending tyranny of the Palace of Crystal, the emerging temptation beckoning all contemporary political regimes. To do so, as Dostoevsky has also already shown, is to succumb to the 'ressentiment' against the promise of meaningful human existence.

Scheler recoils from this avenue of enquiry. He is content to ascribe the 'ressentiment' tendencies of aspiring democracies to a breakdown of the feudal structure that governed the spirit of an earlier age, where each man and class of person knew, in advance, its appointed place in the divine scheme of things:

"The medieval peasant prior to the 13th century does not compare himself to the feudal lord, nor does the artisan compare himself to the knight ... such periods are dominated by the idea that everyone has his 'place' which has been assigned to him by God and nature in which he has his personal duty to fulfill ... From the king down to the hangman and the prostitute, everyone is 'noble' in the sense that he considers himself as irreplaceable."[133]

This, for Scheler, is the fragile rim of history which the wheel of 'ressentiment' has broken through. The ascending age of 'ressentiment' has come about because now no "place is more than a transitory point ... aspirations are intrinsically *boundless* ... the progression of time is interpreted as 'progress' "[134]. Just as in all previous cases, Scheler submerges his enquiry at the moment he promises to break through to its ontological dimension. We shall have to wait upon the reconstruction of Nietzsche's analysis to understand the ground from out of which the "ages" unfolded as expressions of 'ressentiment', including the feudal hierarchy so nostalgically described by Scheler.

Unperturbed, Scheler has dealt out a solution to the problematic phenomenon of 'ressentiment' for all ages, groups, and individuals. It is to that solution that we shall now turn our attention.

E. Love and Ressentiment

If there is a mode of being that truly corresponds to the authentic Christian concept of love *sans ressentiment*, then, in order to live without 'ressentiment', one must become a Christian. This is the hypothesis Max Scheler sets out to prove in proposing an existential solution to the problematic phenomenon of 'ressentiment'.

Scheler commences his 'apologia' of the Christian concept of love, 'agape', by distinguishing it from the Greek concept of 'eros'.

Scheler maintains that there are several defective and interrelated assumptions upon which the Greek concept of love (eros) depends.

First, 'eros' is represented by Scheler as stemming solely from lack or need. It is, therefore, held to be a privative mode of being[135]. Secondly, it is held to be inferior to such eternal excellences as "logical form", "law", "justice" and *agon* or struggle. In the third place 'eros' is asserted to be "the natural corollary of the extremely questionable ancient division of human nature into 'reason' and 'sensuality', into a part that is formative and one that is formed"[136]. In all of these respects 'eros' is held by Scheler to be inferior to 'agape', provisionally characterized as "love . . . explicitly placed above the rational domain — love 'that makes more blessed than all reason' (Augustine)"[137].

Scheler's depiction of the Greek concept of 'eros' is remarkably cavalier and in need of immediate clarification. Typically, he introduces his remarks with the statement: "A brief summary, without reference to specific sources, will be sufficient here."[138] In the context of his discussion of 'eros' Scheler addresses himself almost exclusively only to Plato's 'Symposium'[139]. Given Scheler's claim that 'agape' is superior to 'eros' in just the three respects mentioned above, and that agapistic love alone can overcome 'ressentiment', it is imperative that we examine the evidence, concerning 'eros', upon which Scheler stakes his claim.

To begin with, 'eros' is, as Socrates makes clear in his refutation of Agathon, born not only out of a need for that which one lacks (poverty), but desire for the good longed for and experienced as absent: "Love is the desire for the perpetual possession of the good."[140] 'Ressentiment', as explained by Scheler, would, from the Socratic perspective, represent a dynamic inversion of 'eros', grudging that which it does not possess (because, deeming it good and inaccessible) and experiencing its attractive lure, therefore, in the guise of suffering rather than happiness. Envy and the desire for revenge would, thus, replace plenty and poverty, respectively, as the parents of illegitimate 'eros', i.e., 'ressentiment'. 'Eros', understood as the horizon within which 'ressentiment' moves cannot be ruled defective on the basis of Scheler's groundless assertion that is exclusively a privative mode of being.

Next, we must take up Scheler's second and third allegations, i.e., 2) 'eros' is inferior to other Platonic excellences; 3) 'eros' belongs to a categorical distinction between 'reason' and 'sensuality'. The speech of Socrates, which Plato puts in the mouth of Diotima in the 'Symposium', casts doubt on both assumptions.

First, 'eros' is attracted by one beautiful, concrete, corporeal being. As it matures, it recognizes that this one being merely partakes in the concept of beauty which informs all beings of their beauty. Here 'eros' is governed from an Homeric perspective by the goddess Aphrodite. It is to this sphere of 'eros' that the romantic love described by Phaedrus, in the opening speech of the 'Symposium', belongs. The instability of this domain shows its own limitations either through experience or education. Unlike the uneducable Paris, 'eros' is open to the possibility of further maturation, which means a longing to possess a more suitable companion to satisfy its ardor. The desire for beauty in the corporeal domain is not, however, left behind altogether.

Rather, it moves from the sphere of the private, the volatile, and the hidden into the light of day of the marketplace. Here the goddess Hera exercises supervision. Beauty now appears through the refracted light of honor and recognition. In the same manner that beauty inspires a desire for progeny on the corporeal level, now 'eros' demands a subtler and more enduring kind of immortality. The political life with its honors and triumphs provides a more satisfactory monument to the now transformed desire of eros to live in perpetuity. However, the praise and blame bestowed upon political persons and their actions is dependent upon the esteem given by others. This mode of immortality tends to dim as the eyes grow old and the feats that inspire impassioned enthusiasm grow cold.

Scheler keenly understands, and has brilliantly described, what happens when misbegotten 'eros' turns against itself as the monster child, 'ressentiment', on the corporeal rung and at the rung of political honor. However, his failure to understand the ontological horizon within which 'eros' moves, longing for the immortality it lacks, has concealed the temporal character of the continuity of both the unfolding of 'eros' and its inversion, 'ressentiment'.

This is most revealing in Scheler's failure to grasp the role of 'eros', for Plato, in relation to philosophy. For, 'eros' comes in contact with the most adequate expression of its desire, for Plato, only when it arrives at the deathless ideas — those ideas which cannot be overturned by the corruptibility of sentiments, or the whimsical nature of changing political regimes. Here beauty manifests itself in its most enduring form. The movement from the particular to the general recapitulates itself, moving from one beautiful form to the interrelated totality of forms. One's passion is now for justice, and then for the relationship of justice to the whole scheme of *eide*. The only adequate object fully expressive of the desire for 'eros' to live now and perpetually is *sophia* or wisdom whose protectress is Athena. The relationship of *philia* or authentic friendship in quest of the good which wisdom brings is the very essence of Socratic-Platonic philosophy.

Scheler's failure to comprehend the meaning of 'eros' for the Platonic Socrates, particularly in its relation to philosophy, leaves questions which remain unasked and, therefore, unanswered by his analysis, and which we must address to him. However, the positive thrust of Scheler's analysis must first be allowed to emerge unimpeded.

After having taken 'Greek' love to task for making a distinction of a hard and presumably fast sort between "reason" and "sensuality", Scheler goes on to assert the manifest supremecy of the dualistic metaphysics of Christian love:

" 'Agape' and 'caritas' are sharply, and dualistically separated from 'eros' and 'amor', whereas the Greeks and Romans — though they do acknowledge distinctions in value — rather see a continuity between these types of love. Christian love is a spiritual intentionality which transcends the natural sphere, defeating and superceding the psychological mechanism of the natural instincts (such as hatred against one's enemies, revenge, and desire for retaliation). It can place a man in a completely new state of life . . . the most important difference between the ancient and Christian views of love lies in the direction of its movement."[141]

The principal difference between Greek and Christian love for Scheler lies in the intentional direction from 'lower' to 'higher' in the case of the former and from 'higher' to 'lower' in the case of the latter.

Perceptively, Scheler points to a profound difference in the Greek and Christian versions of the identity and relation of lover to beloved. Scheler correctly asserts that in the Greek view, it is the beloved who is understood as "always nobler and more perfect". Scheler cites as a paradigm case Aristotle's unmoved mover, who summons all beings towards a complete state of *energeia*. Scheler captures the essential spirit of the Aristotelian concept of love:

"The universe is a great chain of dynamic spiritual entities, of forms of being ranging from the 'prima materia' up to man — a chain in which the lower always strives for and is attracted by the higher, which never turns back but aspires upward in its turn. This process continues up to the diety, which itself does not love, but represents the eternally unmoving and unifying *goal* of all these aspirations of love."[142]

The fundamental change in the movement of love in the Christian conception consists, according to Scheler, in the reversal of the relation between lover and beloved, 'higher' and 'lower', creature and Creator[143]. Scheler's explanation for this reversal of movement is alternatively theological, cosmological, and phenomenological. The theological argument affirms the orthodox Hebraic and Christian insistence upon creation *ex nihilo* by a perfect deity. Scheler offers a common, but unsubstantiated ancillary premise that God creates the world out of love. "The eternal 'first mover' of the world is replaced by the 'creator' who created it 'out of love'."[144]

Scheler should rather have said that he will demonstrate that the creator — God of the 'Book of Genesis' — must have created the world out of love. The Biblical text is more spare in its account of creation. Nowhere does it say that on any of the first days God created out of love. Rather, the text states that after each act of creation, upon the six days of fashioning the world, God looked at his creation and said that it was good (*tov*). In summing up His outlook toward creation on the sixth day, the text states simply: "And God saw everything that He had made, and behold, it was very good (*tov moed*)."[145] The simple restatement of the language of the text does not, of course, settle the theological paradox first advanced by Plato in the 'Euthyphro': "Is that which is holy loved by the gods because it is holy, or is it holy because it is loved by the gods?"[146]. Here the riddle posed at the vortex of the 'Euthyphro' may be transposed as follows: 'Was the world created by God because creation was good, or was it deemed good because it was created by God?'.

Scheler's founding cosmological assumption is that the riddle must be answered on the side of affirming that creation is good because, and only because, it is created by God:
"The Christian diety is a *personal* God who created the 'world' out of an infinite overflow of love — not because he wanted to help anyone or anything, for 'nothing' existed before, but only to express his superabundance of love. This new notion of the diety is the conceptual theological expression of the changed attitude toward life."[147]

Scheler's assertion that God creates out of love serves to intensify the philosophical paradox of explaining creation *ex nihilo*, while preserving the concept of divine perfection. Assuming that the One does create out of overflowing love, how is this accomplished without causing contraction or diminution on the part of the One, or without assuming that the One creates out of lack and is, therefore, lacking in perfection prior to creation?

It is from a phenomenological perspective that the most telling of Scheler's objections is made against the Greek concept of love on behalf of the Christian conception. Scheler's phenomenological description sets out to make two vital distinctions: between need and desire, on the one hand, and between expression and purposiveness, on the other hand. The distinction between need and desire, even though it is not elaborated, is suggestive, and upon reflection, compelling. Scheler's remarks here are worth quoting *in toto*:

"How strongly did Neo-Platonic criticism stress that love is a form of 'need' and 'aspiration' which indicates 'imperfection', and that it is false, presumptuous, and sinful to attribute it to the deity! But there is another great innovation: in the Christian view, love is a non-sensuous act of the *spirit* (not a mere state of feeling, as for the moderns), but it is nevertheless not a striving and desiring, and even less a need ... These acts consume themselves in the realization of the desired goal. Love, however, *grows* in its action. And there are no longer any rational principles, any rules or justice higher than love independent of it and preceding it, which should guide its action and its distribution among men according to their value. All are worthy of love — friends and enemies, the good and evil, the noble and the common."[148]

The language Scheler employs to describe the phenomenon of love, as opposed to 'need', 'desire', and 'aspiration' struggles against the assumption taken from Plato where 'desire' and 'need' are themselves not carefully distinguished[149]. Scheler's point is that love, by nature, is different from need and desire in that the attainment of its object increases the power of love rather than signifying its death.

Subsequently, Emmanuel Levinas elaborates on this same theme contrasting "need" and "metaphysical desire", the latter corresponding to Scheler's concept of love:

"The metaphysical desire does not rest upon any prior kinship. It is a desire that cannot be satisfied. For we speak lightly of desires satisfied, or of sexual needs, or even of moral and religious needs. Love itself is thus taken to be the satisfaction of a sublime hunger. If this language is possible, it is because most of our desires and love, too, are not too pure. The desires one can satisfy resemble metaphysical desire only in the deceptions of non-satisfaction or in the exasperation of non-satisfaction and desire which constitutes voluptuosity itself. The metaphysical desire has another intention; it desires beyond everything that can simply complete it. It is like goodness — the desired does not fulfill it, but deepens it."[150]

The point of this comparison is to emphasize the more radical nature of Scheler's characterization of love, which, unlike that of Levinas's concept of metaphysical desire, is not summoned forth towards the beloved. Rather, as Scheler presents it, authentic love is *sui generis* and arises in a wholly gratuitous, and from a philosophical point of view, seemingly inexplicable origin. What, we may ask Scheler, summons forth the direction of the movement of agapistic love when it cannot be the beloved? Moreover, how does Scheler propose to speak of "movement" that is different from mere "motion" when the ground for distinguishing lover and beloved has been collapsed? In any case, a priori in advance of any movement, all obstacles in the path of Scheler's version of agapistic love have been nullified. The longing for expression of such love cannot be blocked, for the goal of love is simply its own expression. Therefore, agapistic love is, we may infer, secured from the hermeneutical circle of 'ressentiment'.

Scheler's implied argument depends, however, on essential assumptions which must now be spelled out in greater detail and reexamined. Scheler maintains that authentic love is the highest good than which there can be no greater:

"There is no longer any 'highest good' independent of and beyond the *act* and movement of love! Love itself is the highest of all goods! The *summum bonum* is no longer the value of a thing, but of an act, the value of love itself *as love* — not for its results and achievements. Indeed the achievements of love are only symbols and proofs of its *presence in the person*."[151]

From a logical point of view, Scheler's assertion that the act of love is that good than which there can be no greater presents a formidable paradox. The position assumes that the highest good is other than the Good itself. It is open to the complaint that G.E. Moore lodges against any attempt to predicate of the good an attribute that could essentially define it without assuming an intuition of the essence of the subject in the act of predication. That is to say, as Moore does, only the predicate "good" can serve to finally define good in an ultimate sense[152].

If authentic love is truly to serve as the remedy to 'ressentiment', then we must make every effort to understand the intention and meaning, as well as the obvious deficiencies of Scheler's argument. The dominant question now before us is this: What does it mean to love such that to love truly is to overcome 'ressentiment'? Can agapistic love overcome the dynamic movement of the spinning wheel of ressentiment?

From a phenomenological point of view, the most fruitful suggestion that Scheler makes is, as we have seen, to distinguish between the phenomenon of "sensible expression" and that of a purposive idea. It must be pointed out that this distinction is introduced only within a theological context which treats of the nature of human love in relation to that of divinity. Assuming the existence of a creator God whose full manifestation is represented in the person of Jesus taken as the Christus, Scheler asks the question of why anyone should love such a God:

"We should not love God because of his heaven and earth: We should love heaven and earth because they are God's and because they adumbrate eternal love by means of sensible *expression* rather than as purposive idea. The same is true for the concept of God."[153]

In context, Scheler's position can be sustained from a theological point of view, if and only if, the God of whom Scheler speaks is identical with and exhausted by the characterization that He is pure love. Otherwise, one would be secretly holding to the position that man loves God for an ulterior purpose, i.e., that it is good to love the world because it is God's, because God is good.

The same problem poses itself in another guise in rethreading our way through Scheler's reliance upon his amended theory of creation *ex nihilo* out of love. If the One does create out of a superabundance of love, and this act of love is understood as sensible expression, then the One and its expression of love must either be distinguished, in which case they are two and not one, or there was never a time prior to the expression of love from the One. In the latter case, then, there can be no creation *ex nihilo*. While these difficulties, of course, apply to any orthodox theory of creation *ex nihilo*, we are reconsidering these difficulties in the light of Scheler's distinction between need and desire, on the one hand, and sensible expression and purposive idea, on the other. We find such distinctions impotent to deal with the assertion of creation *ex nihilo*, out of love, construed as sensible expression.

The injunction to love "the good and the bad", "the just and the sinners", "one's friends and one's enemies", Scheler claims, has its origin in "the idea that love has its origin in God himself"[154]. The theologically implicit claim is one of *imitatio dei*. It seeks to expand the capacity to love beyond the intention toward the profitable, the prudent, the reasonable, and even the good, to the whole of creation and, thereby, to break the bounded love of what, to Scheler's mind, is the limited concept of love in pharisaical Judaism, as well as of Greek antiquity. Scheler comments:

"The ancient precept of loving the good and the just, and of hating the evil and the unjust, is now rejected as 'pharisaism'. Indeed, in a wider metaphysical context, God is not only the 'creator' (instead of a mere ideal, a perfect being, the goal of the world's upward movement), but even the 'creator out of love'. His creation, the 'world' itself, is nothing but the momentary coagulation of an infinitely flowing gesture of love."[155]

If it is logically hard to fathom how the God whom Scheler speaks of could have created in the manner in which Scheler speaks, it is all the more difficult to comprehend in the case of a finite being.

First of all, we should have to know more clearly what is meant by the concept of sensible expression. The implication is that there can be and are actions which are non-intentional in character, i.e. to use Husserlian language, that there is an activity of noesis which proceeds in the absence of noematic objects. This thesis is not wholly implausible and has found an advocate in Levinas, who argues that the concept of intentionality is not exhaustive of human actions. From both a Socratic-Platonic and an Husserlian perspective, the problem posed by Scheler's depiction of love as a mode of sensible expression, or pure act, is not an adequate response to the questions of thematization or quiddity. The moment one demands a true definition of love from Scheler, one makes the wholly reasonable demand that the answer be framed in terms of criteria that will satisfy the quest for meaningfulness, universality, apodicticity, imperishability, and so on. The peculiar problem with Scheler's assertion that authentic love consists in sensible expression stems from his earlier insistence on its spiritual and non-sensuous character, which in turn appears to make the question of quiddity all the more urgent, given the necessarily non-sensous character of "sensible expression" on Scheler's account.

Levinas, who poses theoretical questions of a penetrating sort to the Husserlian concept of intentionality, offers brilliant, concrete descriptions of the manner in which love resists thematization of an eidetic sort and yet can be spoken of as manifesting sensible expression. To cite only an illustration, consider his characterization of the caress:

"The caress consists in seizing upon nothing, in soliciting what ceaselessly escapes its form toward a future never future enough, in soliciting what slips away as though it *were not yet*. It *searches*, it forages. It is not an intentionality of disclosure but of search: a movement unto the invisible. In a certain sense it *expresses* love, but suffers from an inability to tell it. It is hungry for this very expression, in an unremitting increase of hunger. It thus goes further than to its term, it aims beyond an existent however future, which, precisely as an *existent*, knocks already at the gates of being ... The caress aims at neither a person nor a thing. It loses itself in a being that dissipates as though into an impersonal dream without will and even without resistance, a passivity, an already animal or infantile anonymity, already entirely at death ... The caress does not *act*, does not grasp possibles. ... Its 'intention' no longer goes forth unto the *light*, unto the meaningful. Wholly passion, it is compassion for the passivity, the suffering, the evanescence of the tender."[156]

The extensive citation from Levinas only suggests the possibility of elaborating a theme that Scheler characteristically introduces almost as a pause between sentences in a conversation. While Levinas's description of the caress belongs to the phenomenology of 'eros' (or perhaps 'caritas') rather than 'agape', and while there are important and foundational differences with Scheler's account of authentic love, the relevant considerations belong to the shared view that love can appear, at least in one of its modes, as expressive of sensibility, while moving towards a transcendance of the sensible.

Provisionally granting Scheler's assumption that it is possible to speak of authentic love as expressional rather than intentional, we must ask how love does express itself such that there will no longer be grounds for experiencing injury as unwarranted and unanswerable, and thus depriving 'ressentiment' of the soil necessary for it to grow and flourish.

Scheler considers the case of Saint Francis of Assisi, who plunged whole-heartedly into the most abject kind of human suffering out of the impulse of authentic agapistic love. Scheler properly takes issue with the kind of reduction which Nietzsche carries on with respect to all asceticism linked with caring for the wretched. He maintains that

Saint Francis does not love sickness and poverty as such, but "what is *behind* them, and his help is directed *against* these evils"[157]. This is not, as in the case of modern humanism, a relishing of the morbid because it is morbid, and in that sense it is not necessarily a 'ressentiment' phenomenon. Scheler says of Saint Francis: "When Francis of Assisi kisses festering wounds and does not even kill the bugs that bite him, but leaves his body to them as a(n) hospitable home ... [most] people saw something bug-like in everything that lives, whereas Francis sees the holiness of 'life' even in the bug."[158]

It is imperative for Scheler to insist that authentic love seeks to derive no utilitarian benefit for oneself or apparently even for the other. It is only the "fake love of 'ressentiment' man", the love of modern humanism that has falsified authentic love and married it to the concept of utilitarian benefit. All such 'ressentiment' love which Scheler perjoratively calls "altruism" masks hatred:

"Thus the 'altruistic' urge is really a form of hatred, of self-hatred, *posing* as its opposite ('Love') in the false perspective of consciousness. In the same way, in *ressentiment* morality, love for the 'small', the 'poor', the 'weak', and the 'oppressed' is really disguised hatred, repressed envy, an impulse to detract, etc., directed against he opposite phenomena: 'wealth', 'strength', 'power' ("largess"). When hatred does not dare to come out into the open, it can be easily expressed in the form of ostensible love − love for something which has featured the opposite of those of the hated object."[159]

While Scheler admits that there are passages in the New Testament, especially in the 'Gospel of Luke', that must be treated as expressions of 'ressentiment' love ("It is easier for a camel to go through a needle's eye than for a rich man to enter into the kingdom of God."), he affirms the reality of authentic love by suggesting that there are ways of assisting others free of 'ressentiment'. Scheler explains the preoccupation of Jesus and his followers with the poor, the sick, the wretched, etc.:

"This is truly no temptation by the pleasures of sin, nor a demoniacal love for its 'sweetness' nor the attraction of the forbidden or the lure of novel experiences. It is an outburst of tempestuous love and tempestuous compassion for *all* men who are felt as *one*, indeed for the universe as a whole; a love which makes it seem frightful that only some should be 'good', while the others are 'bad' and reprobate. In such moments, love and a deep *sense of solidarity* are repelled by the thought that we alone should be 'good', together with some others.

This fills us with a kind of loathing for those who can accept this privilege, and we have an urge to move away from them."[160]

It is the undifferentiated character of agapistic love as conceptualized by Scheler that at once seems to represent the source of its greatest appeal and at the same time poses hard and seemingly unanswerable questions. The reach which Scheler ascribes to authentic Christian love is sweeping, even universal in its scope. In advance of all thematization it takes up a stance that offers the appearance of overcoming the source of all unwarranted suffering.

Paradoxically, as characterized by Scheler, authentic love frees one from dependence upon the other — the assumed source of all suffering. In advance, it renders the other powerless to take away the gift of expressing love, and, therefore, of mending ever again the rent in the garment of human existence. It does so, as Scheler would have it, by recognizing that in the commandment to love one's enemies, one already recognizes that one has enemies, and, therefore, does not deny exteriority even in the moment of transcending the threats that emanate from it.[161] Limitless love expresses a recognition of the limitations of human finitude and yet is given the gift of self-transcendance.

How is agapistic love, which, for Scheler, bypasses the way of philosophy, to resolve the problem of philosophy? How does this boundless love express itself within the multiply experienced limitations of human finitude? How, for beings who are situated spatially within limited horizons, does the limitless love spend itself? How, for a being who faces in one direction rather than another, do criteria of selectivity emerge when this love that has beneficiaries without benefits expresses itself now to one and then to another?

To whom shall one turn first, the lame, the halt, or the blind, the lepers, or to those who immediately present themselves before the eyes turned toward them? And how shall one know, now in the present, or how shall one learn, when there is no time except for the incessant expression of love? And how shall those who are not near at hand and those who do not dwell nearby, and those who will need a love that has not spent itself too quickly, for their moment may not yet have come, how shall such love be tempered so that it may be sustained[162]?

How shall love, that good than which there is no greater, inform the content of the hierarchy of values which Scheler so adamantly insists has been subverted by all the modern off-shoots that have falsely arisen to claim the title to authentic Christian love: humanism, liberalism, socialism of every kind[163]?

When one denies the reality of scarcity as, in any way, compromising the aspiration of limitless love, then the command to love loses its urgency. Or, why shall we say that even Jesus chose to turn his attention to the poor, the sick, the wretched? Is love to be understood in such a way that the upsurge of its spontaneous giving, raw and aboriginal, is not to meet the expression of justice where self-limitation is demanded and self-retraint commanded? Is creation itself to become disdained as a mere impediment on the way to loving it as though man were not assigned the role of creature, as keeper and redeemer of all the earth? It is no wonder that Scheler speaks with such 'ressentiment' about the "avenging God of the original testament", or of his sacred commandments that recognize and legislate the steps to be taken lovingly in the accomplishment of a just order which unfolds as so many days and nights, weeks and months, and years in a sacred time.

As Scheler explains the concept of agapistic love, the ontic expression of its content masks a deep and abiding ontological 'ressentiment' against the inability to express itself *once* and *for all*. The absent others, the absent future, the absent past, the absent One, just insofar as they do not fully manifest their presence, are held in deepest contempt. Agapistic love, as explained by Scheler, arrests the wheel of 'ressentiment' only by depriving creation of the power to become. It cannot be set in motion by 'eros', nor is it capable of transformation into philosophy.

F. Conclusion and Transition

The same failure of analysis, prefigured in Scheler's phenomenological method, the concealing of the ontological dimension of 'ressentiment', has doomed his solution as well. Scheler wished to distinguish 'agape' from both 'eros' and the "altruism" of secular humanism in such a manner as to demonstrate that 'agape' was free of 'ressentiment'. We have already shown that Scheler's presentation of the concept of 'agape' misconstrues the Socratic-Platonic concept of 'eros', and that it fails to secure 'agape' against the charge of ontological 'ressentiment'.

Nietzsche has already argued more convincingly that the "fake love" of secular humanism represents the inescapable development of 'agape' with its wellsprings in 'ressentiment'. For Nietzsche, the 'ressentiment' concealed in 'agape' is but one important stage in the historicity of existence, whose reflection can be seen most clearly in the birth and unfolding of western philosophy. It is to that story, and Nietzsche's recounting of it, that we shall now turn our attention.

III. THE ONTOLOGY OF 'RESSENTIMENT': NIETZSCHE

A. Prologue: The Birth of Philosophy from Out of the Spirit of Revenge

The ultimate source of all 'ressentiment', the rancor against time itself, originates for Nietzsche, with the birth of philosophy. In the single utterance attributed to Anaximander of Miletus, Nietzsche discovers the first metaphysical reflection of 'ressentiment'. Nietzsche's meditation on the dawn of 'ressentiment' in western thought is offered in his first significant work, the posthumously published 'Philosophy in the Tragic Age of the Greeks'[164].

The utterance credited to Anaximander, and reflected upon by Nietzsche, reads as follows:

"Where the source of things is, to that place they must also pass away, according to necessity, for they must pay penance and be judged for their injustices, in accordance with the ordinance of time."[165]

The core of Nietzsche's interpretation of Anaximander's statement is stunning in its simplicity. Anaximander discovered the primary structure of transience. All beings come-to-be fated to pass away. The "ordinance of time" mandates the coming-to-be and passing away of all beings. All beings are, therefore, contingent. The "ordinance of time" is a necessary truth legislating the actual appearance of beings.

Anaximander understood the terrifying consequences of his discovery. Transience itself is the irremediable, and primary, injury responsible for all suffering:

"Whence that restless, caeseless coming-into-being and giving birth, whence that grimace of painful disfiguration on the countenance of nature, whence the never ending dirge in all realms of existence."[166]

If Anaximander had stopped here, according to Nietzsche, the ruling beginnings of philosophy would have charted a path to unconcealed truth.

Anaximander, however, could not abide the truth of his own discovery. There must be a *reason* to explain the suffering imposed by the "ordinance of time". Nietzsche asks the question which he believes Anaximander himself must have asked: "How can anything pass away which has the right to be?"[167] The answer Anaximander gives is that beings must "be judged for their injustices"[168]. Passing away is the penance paid for the injustice of having come-to-be. For, nothing has the right to be. Coming-to-be is an illegitimate emancipation from the unbroken calm of eternity. In advance of every deed, and all coming-to-be, expiation is commanded, the expiation of persihing.

According to Nietzsche, Anaximander has recoiled from his own profound discovery. He intuited the primary governing structure of a universe indifferent to the concerns and aspirations of being human. There is, therefore, no justification given for existence.

Anaximander experienced an inexpungeable guilt simultaneously with the apprehension of the senseless suffering imposed by transience. A primordial hesitation thwarted the will-to-become. The remedy was found in superimposing an ethical drama upon an ontological datum. "From this world of injustice, of insolent apostasy from the primeval one-ness of all things, Anaximander flees into a metaphysical fortress from which he leans out, letting his gaze sweep the horizon. At last after long pensive silence he puts a question to all creatures: 'What is your existence worth? And, if it is worthless why are you here? Your guilt, I see, causes you to tarry in your existence'."[169]

As quietly as a leaf buffeted in the cool breeze of night time, Anaximander submerged the grudge which emerged from the senseless suffering inflicted on man by the hands on the clock of time. To *become* means, for Anaximander, to "tarry" in existence, to begrudge the journey home, to eternity. It is "insolent apostasy", a way of postponing penance, justice, perishing.

The rancor against the ordinance of time delivers, out of the spirit of revenge, the aboriginal devaluation of existence, that is to become the subterranean and controlling structure in the historicity of philosophy. It will take Nietzsche many years to resolve the riddle he poses in concluding his meditation on Anaximander: "Who is there that could redeem you from the curse of coming-to-be?"[170]

The historicity of 'ressentiment' culminates, for Nietzsche, in the phenomenon of European nihilism, the time of his own generation. It is signified in the death of all absolutes and the inability to believe in anything at all, the time expressed by Dostoevsky's man from the underground, as requiring one to make up a life for oneself so as at least to be able to live in some way.

The advent of nihilism is determined in the threefold devaluation of transience by: 1) the "Socratic" transvaluation of the values of the world of the Homeric Greeks; 2) the "other-worldliness" that

Nietzsche associates with the elaboration of the Socratic devaluation; and 3) the advent and ascendancy of Christendom, in which the world outlook of the West in the two milennia, culminating in nihilism, is sealed. It is necessary before proceeding to offer a brief reflection on the method and aim of Nietzsche's investigation, the criterion which served to guide his enquiry and the goal at which it is directed.

B. The Historicity of 'Ressentiment'

1. Problem of Method

The development of philosophy from out of the "spirit of revenge" proceeds, for Nietzsche, from out of an understanding of human suffering wrought by the rancor against time and from a desire for deliverance from it. His exploration of 'ressentiment' advances strictly according to the criteria he set forth in 'The Use and Abuse of History' where he explains the three kinds of history of which the philosophers make use: the "monumental", the "antiquarian", and the "critical": "History is necessary to the living man in three ways: in relation to his action and struggle (monumental), his conservatism and reverence (antiquarian), his suffering and desire for deliverance (critical)."[171]

The philosopher puts monumental and antiquarian history in the service of the critical. He recognizes that the factical appearances of the present live from the great turning points in the deeds and ideas of the past. He recollects the living history of the past within an understanding of its enduring character in the present, but he "must have the strength to break up the past, and apply it, too, in order to live"[172].

At times Nietzsche, in his reconstruction of the development of philosophy out of 'ressentiment', appears to give "antiquarian" history short shrift. For example, the philosophy of Plato is reduced to the "other-worldliness" associated with Platonism. His portrayal of Socrates in "The Problem of Socrates" draws heavily and most polemically upon the Platonic description of the death of Socrates in the 'Phaedo'. The portrait of Jesus found in the 'Anti-Christ' and the incredibly harsh treatment of Pauline Christianity offer assertions which Nietzsche makes almost no attempt to ground in textural or historical evidence.

It is the character of 'ressentiment' in the present, reflected in the image of Dostoevsky's man from the underground, and described by

Scheler, that demands an ontological explanation. As Nietzsche remarks: *"You can explain the past only by what is most powerful in the present."*[173] It is the inner history of the purified reflection of 'ressentiment' in its very unfolding that Nietzsche's radical phenomenology sets out to describe:

". . . the 'super-historical' philosopher sees all the history of nations and individuals from within. He has a divine insight into the original meaning of the hieroglyphs, and comes to be weary of the letters that are continually unrolled before him."[174]

It is the inner history, the historicity of 'ressentiment' that Nietzsche, in uncovering, opens to an ontological investigation.

The first section of the present chapter demonstrates the decisive philosophical transformation in the historicity of 'ressentiment' as presented by Nietzsche. It prepares the way for Nietzsche's original reflection on the ontological ground responsible for the historicity of 'ressentiment'. Here we present Nietzsche engaging in the movement which Heidegger is later to characterize as expressing the philosophic bridge between the inner history of being human (*Dasein*) and the temporal ground of its actual appearance.

"In analyzing the historicality of Dasein we shall try to show that this entity is not 'temporal' because it 'stands in history' but that, on the contrary, it exists historically and can so exist only because it is temporal in the very basis of its Being."[175]

Not surprisingly, it is Heidegger's own work, 'What is Called Thinking?' that has served to focus attention on the ontological dimension of the rancor against time in Nietzsche's thought. Heidegger's meditation on Nietzsche has opened to questioning the reflection set out in the second section of the present chapter. Subsequently, it is to Heidegger's own thought that we shall move to remedy the defects in Nietzsche's resolution to the question he first asks of Anaximander: "Who is there who could redeem you from the curse of coming-to-be?"[176]

2. The Development of Philosophy out of 'Ressentiment'
a) The Socratic Turn

Nietzsche represents Socrates as the decisive figure in the history of 'ressentiment'. In the 'Twilight of the Idols' Nietzsche offers a reflection on the problem of Socrates that radicalizes a reflection set in motion in the 'Birth of Tragedy'. Socrates is represented as the consummation and decline of the world outlook that governed the Greek spirit from Homer to Aeschylus. At the same time, he is held to pre-figure the emerging Platonic vision of reality which is to dominate all subsequent philosophy. It is Socrates, on Nietzsche's account, who prepares the ground out of which emerges the "other-worldliness" which Nietzsche associates with Platonic metaphysics. The "other-worldliness" of Platonic metaphysics is the logical metaphysical out-come for Nietzsche of Socrates's view that life is essentially "to be sick a long time"[177]. Nietzsche charges that Socrates, the patron saint of philosophy, devalues the meaning of being human and that Plato enthrones other-worldliness to justify that devaluation.

In the first of the twelfe sections devoted to the "Problem of Socrates" in the 'Twilight of the Idols', Nietzsche classifies Socrates as belonging to that class of persons he characterizes as "the wisest men of all ages"[178]. He sets Socrates at a distance from the other members of that class: "Even Socrates said, as he died: 'To live — that means to be sick a long time: I owe Aesculapius the Savior a rooster.' Even Socrates tired of it. What does that evidence?"[179] Nietzsche's posing of "The Problem of Socrates" is this: How can the wisest of mortals be a slanderer of human life who believes that life is best characterized as "a lengthy sickness"?

It is the meaning of the Socratic enterprise of calling into ques-tion the essences of existence that Nietzsche challenges. When the values of human existence, and life itself, are rendered problemati-cal from a philosophic standpoint, one has already conceded that the claiming power of existence has been drained of its authority. "Good" can be predicated of human life in a meaningful way, Nietzsche im-plies, only when the denial of this assertion is no longer treated as an existential absurdity.

Nietzsche asserts: *"That the value of life cannot be estimated.*[180]*"* Who is in a position to make a dispassionate judgment concerning the value of (human) life? The living are excluded on the basis that they are interested parties rather than proper judges; "the dead, for a dif-ferent reason"[181]. That he has presented himself with an existential contradiction that makes even an affirmative judgment impossible appears to bother him not at all[182]. Philosophical questioning con-cerning the value of human life evidences the declining power of life. The persons who pose such questions are considered to be decadents, and Socrates, the wisest of all, is hence characterized as the most decadent.

Nietzsche regards Socratic dialectic as at once "anti-Greek' and an emblematic symptom of decline. Corresponding to the degeneration of the values, immediately and apodictically apprehend as informing the foundation of the Homeric world, and the authentic Greek spirit manifest in this world, is a distrust of the reliability of intuition. The axiological correlative of epistemic intuition is represented, by Nietzsche, as authority, expressed through the mode of command in the realm of ethical action. Nietzsche rejects the view that the Platonic Socrates made unqualified philosophic progress in freeing human reason from dependence upon religious and political authority. The dialectical method, as Nietzsche would have it, not only betrays an absence of trust in intuition and command, but sets out to devalue their reliability and authority. It, thereby, weakens the apprehension of certainty and rightness asserted to be known in the immediacy of the Homeric world. In the world of the 'Iliad' one knew instinctively what was possessed of value, and the right to compete for it was taken for granted.

Nietzsche asserts that "Wherever authority still forms part of good bearing, where one does not give reasons but commands, the dialectician is a kind of buffoon: One laughs at him, one does not take him seriously. Socrates was the buffoon who *got himself taken seriously*: What really happened there?"[183]

Nietzsche launches his assault on Socratic dialectic from two directions: 1) It is essentially dishonest: "Honest things, like honest men, do not carry their reasons in their hands like that. It is indecent to show all five fingers."[184] It is dishonest because it advances an unwanted necessity as a superior excellence. It is a subtle and invidious way of acknowledging that the naturally superior weapons of self-defense are lacking. Because one lacks the power of authority to enforce one's intuitively apprehended rights through command, one busies one's adversary with ironic questions occasioning his mistrust in the nature of that authority by virtue of which he expresses his power over the questioner. Socratic irony, ever the companion of dialectic, presents the visage of calm serenity as it harbors the outlook of mistrust of self. 2) Until the time of Socrates, dialectic was an ineffectual method "repudiated in good society". Nietzsche augments this assertion by pointing to the fact "nothing is easier to erase than a dialectical effect: the experience of every meeting at which there are speeches proves this"[185].

Out of what weakness, what need for self-defense, is the armor of

Socratic irony taken up? If Socratic dialectic is ineffectual, as Nietzsche claims, how is it that the "Socratic equation of reason, virtue, and happiness"[186] — a conclusion dialectically arrived at by the Platonic Socrates — has managed, as Nietzsche acknowledges, to influence all subsequent philosophy? This historical success is all the more puzzling, if we even provisionally accept Nietzsche's description of this conclusion, as "that most bizarre of all equations, which, moreover, is opposed to all the instincts of the earlier Greeks"[187]? What conditions must have prevailed such that a caricature of the classic Greek hero, a buffoon, *got himself taken seriously*?

According to Nietzsche, two conditions prevailed, merging in the person of Socrates, which permitted this decisive development. First, a plebeian revolt against noble and aristocratic values was under way and in the process of establishing a democracy. On Nietzsche's view, the effort to establish a democratic political order was a symptom of decline because it represented an unwarranted subversion and effective inversion of aristocratic values. Secondly, Socrates was himself ugly in his outward appearance. Nietzsche observes that "ugliness, in itself an objection, is among the Greeks almost a refutation"[188].

The Platonic distinction between appearance and reality, so vital to all subsequent metaphysics, is here understood by Nietzsche as issuing out of the soil of political and personal 'ressentiment'. With the advent of Socrates, "appearance" and "reality" are in the process of being transvalued. Behind the apparent order given by nature is a concealed one that is inversely reflected by the "looks" of the world. The thwarted impulse of political revenge retains its governing intention while altering its expression to one of metaphysical 'ressentiment'.

The hidden agenda of the "real" order is derived dialectically with the aim of wreaking vengeance upon the order of authority embodied in the knowing looks issuing from the faces commanding the direction of the *polis*. In a series of mountingly strident rhetorical questions, Nietzsche tellingly makes his point:

"Is the irony of Socrates an expression of revolt? Of plebeian 'ressentiment?' Does he, as one oppressed, enjoy his own ferocity in the knife-thrusts of his syllogisms? Does he *avenge* himself on the noble people whom he fascinates? As a dialectician, one holds a merciless tool in one's hand; one can become a tyrant by means of it; one compromises those one conquers. The dialectician leaves it to his opponent to prove that he is no idiot: he makes one furious and helpless at the same time.

The dialectician renders the intellect of his opponent powerless. Indeed? Is dialectic only a form of *revenge* in Socrates?"[189]

Through the method of dialectical inquiry, Socrates was able, Nietzsche implies, to insinuate mistrust in both the mode of valuation and to cause suspicion concerning the objects of value both by and within the ruling class. The demand for dialectical proof and demonstration, in weakening the reliance on intuition and command, yields transvaluation and subsequent displacement of reasons for intuition, dialectical question for command, and philosophical wisdom for *agon* and honor.

From the Socratic-Platonic point of view to legislate values in the mode of command — without giving reasons or answering to the objections of reason — represents a refusal to take up the very task of philosophy. It represents an immature reflection of being human that manifests itself in the behavior of a child or a tyrant. What Nietzsche fails to explain, from the Socratic-Platonic viewpoint, is how life, lived in the imperative mode, engages in the activity of self-interpretation. He offers no systematic account of those conditions necessary and sufficient to guarantee either the veracity or validity of his own descriptions.

However, Nietzsche does offer a credible explanation for how Socrates was able to exert an appeal on the very class that he was undertaking to sabotage and disenfranchise: Dialectic preserved the agonistic impulse of the Greeks while transforming its mode of expression. The wrestling match between men gave way to the collision of opposing forces in the realm of speech. Nietzsche states that the source of the appeal of Socrates consisted in the fact that he was 'a great erotic'[190]. Socrates, the erotic, succeeded in sublimating the impulse of 'eros' within the framework of his newly envisioned version of the authentic contest. Upon what basis does Nietzsche draw this conclusion?

It is to dialectical analysis that Nietzsche has recourse in explaining, and partially to justifying, the Socratic enterprise. Socrates knowingly advanced a doctrine resulting in the hypertrophy of the faculty of reason because he recognized that the instincts of old Athens were no longer reliable: "Old Athens was coming to an end. And Socrates understood that all the world *needed* him — his means, his cure, his personal artifice of self-preservation."[191] Socrates recognized in himself, according to Nietzsche, an extreme case of the reflection of an incipient distress with a universal reach: "No one was any longer master over himself, the instincts turned *against* each other."[192] The impulses, once so reliable as a guide for right conduct, had begun to play the tyrant. Socrates, whom Nietzsche characterizes as "a cave of bad appetites"[193], recognized the necessity for mastering himself and the demand to produce a *"counter-tyrant"*[194]. Nietzsche asks a question crucial to his interpretation of Socrates's character: "How did Socrates become master over himself?"[195] For, Nietzsche believed Socrates to be the most extreme embodiment of a time when the "instincts were in anarchy: everywhere one was within five paces of excess: *monstrum in animo* was the general danger."[196]

Socrates diagnosed the remedy as well as the disease harbored within his own person. Socrates fascinated the Greeks with his "awe-inspiring ugliness"[197]. Therefore, he would make an excellence out of a necessity. The previously esteemed meaning of beauty would have to undergo radical transformation[198]. The persona of Socrates conceals the depth of inward beauty of his *psyche*. Socrates, the ugliest of the Greeks in his physical bearing, succeeded, through the transvaluation of values born of 'ressentiment', in satisfying his own unquenchable 'eros' by making himself the object of erotic fascination.

With subtle dialectical precision Nietzsche justifies the Socratic transvaluation of values. Nietzsche, the critic, is also an admirer. He asserts that: "when one finds it necessary to turn *reason* into a tyrant, as Socrates did, the danger cannot be slight that something else will play the tyrant"[199]. It is a dialectically derived conclusion in which Nietzsche is deducing the conditions which must have prevailed for the "wisest of sages" to have had recourse to an otherwise unbalanced and unacceptable alternative. Nietzsche's argument may be transposed into the following syllogism:
1) Socrates was the wisest of sages.
2) Socrates established reason as a tyrant.
3) Therefore, a greater danger would have existed if 2) above was not premised for a warrantable reason.
   Otherwise 1) would not be true.
Nietzsche elaborates his conclusion by appending a description of the existential consequences of concluding otherwise:
"Rationality was then hit upon as the savior; neither Socrates nor his 'patients' had any choices about being rational: It was *de rigeur*, it was their last resort. The fanaticism with which all Greek reflection throws itself upon rationality betrays a desperate situation: there was

danger, there was but one choice: either to perish or — to be *absurdly rational.*"[200]

Nietzsche unabashedly uses Socratic dialectic to inveigh against the origin of that very mode of thinking. He is able to assume his conclusion only if "the wisest of sages" gives "good reasons" for advancing an attack against the instincts and intuitions.

In his presentation of "The Problem of Socrates" Nietzsche can be interpreted as making a merely psychological inquiry out of the personal and subjective motives of Socrates in which both the terms "personal" and "subjective" have perjorative connotations. If Nietzsche were content to point out the physical ugliness of Socrates and ascribe to it Plato's theories on the newly fashioned understanding of the beautiful and the good, we should be able to dismiss Nietzsche's reflections on Socrates as arbitrary and capricious. However, Nietzsche situates his reflections on the persona of Socrates within a generalized consideration of the meaning of dialectical questioning within the life-world of Athens. The power of Nietzsche's portrayal of the role of 'ressentiment' in the life of Socrates permits us to comprehend the dual attraction and repulsion which Socrates held for the *polis* of Athens.

Moreover, his analysis makes clear why Nietzsche recognizes the soil of 'ressentiment' as the only one which permitted Greek spirit a chance of enduring. Nietzsche appreciates, perhaps more deeply than any other modern, that the Socratic revolt on behalf of reason represents the birth of the spirit of scientific understanding, and that it aims at securing a home in being for every man.

"We must not draw back before the question of what such a phenomenon as that of Socrates indicates; for in view of the Platonic dialogues we are certainly not entitled to regard it as merely disintegrating negative force... Once we see clearly how after Socrates, the mystagogue of science, one philosophic school succeeds another, wave upon wave; how the hunger for knowledge reached a never-suspected universality ...; how this universality first spread a common net of thought over the whole globe, actually holding out the prospect of the lawfulness of an entire solar system ... *we cannot fail to see in Socrates the one turning point and vortex of so-called world history.* For if we imagine the whole incalculable sum of energy used up for this world tendency had been used *not* in the service for knowledge but ... i.e., egoistic aims of individuals and peoples, then we realize that in that case universal wars of annihilation and continual migrations of peoples would probably have weakened the instinctive lust for life to such an extent that suicide would have become a general custom."[201]

The description of Socrates expressed in the words above are found in Nietzsche's first book, the 'Birth of Tragedy', published in 1872. "The Problem of Socrates" found in the 'Twilight of the Idols', the last book to be published by Nietzsche himself, in 1889, has radicalized the question of what was concealed in the "one turning point and vortex of so-called history".

The 'Birth of Tragedy' has already made apparent what the Socratic advance had concealed. The birth of the rancor against time, evident in the utterance of Anaximander, has become an axiom in the dialectical revaluation of the meaning of life and death:

"With the torch of this thought in our hands, let us now look at Socrates: he appears to us as the first who could not only live, guided by this instinct of science, but also — and this is far more — die that way. Hence, the image of the *dying Socrates*, as the human being whom knowledge and reasons have liberated from the fear of death, is the emblem that, above the entrance gate of Science, reminds all of its mission — namely, to make existence appear comprehensible and thus justified."[202]

It is no longer simply penance owed that causes beings to pass away. Now, it is *good* that beings pass away; it is the only way of making life "comprehensible and justified".

The rancor against time intuited by Anaximander has been transformed by Socratic dialectic into the 'ressentiment' against existence.

The enthusiasm for life and the dread of death, so evident in the world of the 'Iliad', has been transvalued. There, as Nietzsche describes it,

"Existence . . . is regarded as desirable in itself, and the real pain of Homeric man is caused by parting from it, especially by early parting: so that now, reversing the wisdom of Silenus, we might say of the Greeks that 'to die soon is worst of all for them, the next worst — to die at all'. Once heard, it will ring out again; do not forget the lament of the short-lived Achilles, mourning the leaflike change and vicissitudes of the race of men and the decline of the heroic age. It is not unworthy of the greatest hero to long for the continuation of life even though he live as a day laborer."[203]

The Socratic leap forward concealed the cost of its victory over mounting chaos and the resultant subjugation of the natural world.

The meaning of wisdom and courage were revalued. If one had not the courage to recognize that "as long as life is *ascending*, happiness equals instinct"[204], and a taste for life, now one had the wisdom to die either all at once or to make ready for its advent:

"Did he himself still comprehend this, this most brilliant of all selfout-witters? Was this what he said to himself in the end, in the *wisdom* of his courage to die? Socrates *wanted* to die: not Athens to sentence him. 'Socrates is no physician', he said softly to himself; 'here death alone is the physician. Socrates himself has merely been sick a long time'."[205]

Death has been robbed of its sting and represents release from suffering. Life is revalued as a 'lengthy sickness' to be endured. The first stage in Nietzsche's meta-history of philosophy from out of 'ressentiment' is complete. Man is on his way to becoming estranged from his body, the forces of the natural order, and the life cycle that manifests itself from birth to death.

b. *"Platonism"*

Platonic metaphysics, and all subsequent philosophy in its service, is asserted to be rancorous against sheer becoming and has, through the employement of dialectical reason, based in 'ressentiment', created such fictions as unity, identity, permanence, substance, cause, thinghood, being[206]. The section entitled "Reason in Philosophy", following immediately upon Nietzsche's investigation of "The Problem of Socrates", states the matter most polemically:

"You ask me which of the philosophers' traits are really idiosyncracies? For example, their lack of historical sense, their hatred of the very idea of becoming, their Egypticism. They think that they show their *respect* for a subject when they de-historicize it, *sub specie aeterni* — when they turn it into a mummy. All that philosophers have handled for thousands of years have been concept-mummies; nothing real escaped their grasp alive. When these honorable idolators of concepts worship something, they kill it and stuff it; they threaten the life of everything they worship. Death, old age, as well as procreation and growth are to their minds objections — even refutations. Whatever has being does not become; whatever becomes does not have being. Now they all believe, desperately even, in what has being. But since they never grasp it, they seek for reasons why it is kept from them. 'There must be mere appearance, there must be some deception which prevents us from perceiving that which has being: where is the deceiver?"[207]

How sheer becoming permits the configuration of death, change, old-age, procreation, and growth is not rendered questionable by Nietzsche. The concept of change requires the concept of rest to be made philosophically comprehensible. Yet, Nietzsche does not trouble to explain its possible appearance.

The criterion for distinguishing such falsified reflections from genuine appearance is epistemological rather than metaphysical. In a single formula, Nietzsche restates his epistemological argument: " 'Reason' is the cause of our falsification of the testimony of the senses."[208]

The 'testimony of the senses' is reliable, apparently infallible, in a way in which no one, not even Heraclitus, whose name Nietzsche wished to be linked with, has appreciated. "Insofar as the senses show becoming, passing away, and change, they do not lie."[209] If all the concepts linked to permanence are so many "concept-mummies", then the senses tell all, and do not lie in any respect. The nose is a case in point: "This nose, for example, of which no philosopher has yet spoken with reverence and gratitude, is actually the most delicate instrument at our disposal: it is able to detect minimal differences of motion which even a spectroscope cannot detect."[210] The nose alone can scent generation and decay. Long before the understanding came upon the first recognition of decline, decay is disernible because it can be scented.

Once, with Socrates, dialectical reason knowingly subdued the impressions received through the primary world of the senses for the purpose of legislating a falsified version of reality. Now that the senses have been devalued as a reliable source of understanding, the imposition of a falsified understanding follows more from an obliviosness to the power of sensory apprehension than from premeditated denial. The fate of the philosophic historicity of 'ressentiment' reached its second, decisive devaluation when one had become "out of touch" with the senses.

c) Christianity

The third and last decisive state in the historicity of 'ressentiment' was reached with the advent of Christianity, and sealed with the ascendancy of Christendom. According to Nietzsche, as the 'Anti-Christ' makes

clear, Jesus is the one and only authentic Christian. The very origination of the church he sees as representing an inversion and denial of
the meanings embodied in the life of Jesus.

Nietzsche's treatment of Jesus bears marked similarities to his
interpretation of Socrates. Like Socrates, Jesus is depicted as an
extreme decadent. He sensed that the reigning value structure of
Jewish existence had long since ceased to exert a compelling authority. However, while Socrates was insistent on preparing the way for a
new order through the transvaluation of all previously esteemed
values, Jesus — according to Nietzsche — lives a life of unrecoiling acceptance that affirms the futility of all attempts to transform the
political institutions of everyday life. From an ontic standpoint,
Nietzsche images Jesus as having no vestige or trace of rancor in his
being.

For Nietzsche, Jesus is depicted as overcoming dialectical opposi-
tions, antinomies, and contrasts of every kind. By submitting himself
without holding back or holding secret expectations as to the consequences of such submission, Jesus is depicted by Nietzsche as leading
a life of total affirmation towards fate itself. In Nietzsche's interpretation, Jesus is concerned with establishing the "kingdom of heaven" on
earth. He most accurately reflects his stance towards life in the statement: "I am the way, the truth, and the life."[211] The doctrine of
resurrection is portrayed by Nietzsche as a later falsification introduced by the founders of the church. Moreover, the only significant
aspect of the crucifixion is, for Nietzsche, the manner of unrecoiling
acceptance with which Jesus faces his fate. Here, unspeakable suffering is transformed into bliss by total submission. Jesus does not teach
a future possessed of reality, nor a past that demands atonement. The
promised future is not at hand; it is an accomplished fact.

On Nietzsche's view, this stance of Jesus which affirms all, even
the necessity of unwarranted suffering, is still described as the epi-
tomy of decadence. This is true, for Nietzsche, because Jesus' way of
overcoming the rancor against time still moves within the horizon of
ontological 'ressentiment' by not acknowledging the historicity of
existence. The life of total "Yea-saying" refuses to admit the moment
of dialectical negation and therefore is incapable of selection, decision.
It is thereby dispossessed of past and future.

In the 'Anti-Christ' which, despite its title, gives Nietzsche's most
sympathetic portrait of Jesus, great pains are taken to distinguish
Jesus from his apostles. In fact, according to Nietzsche, Jesus can have

no legitimate apostles. Nietzsche is making a point of logic here rather than theology. The point may be symbolized as follows:

1) Teaching presupposes the ability to make discriminatory judgments.
2) Discriminatory judgments presuppose "nay-saying".
3) Jesus refuses to accept 2).

Ergo, Jesus is not a teacher. Otherwise 1) would be false. Moreover, Jesus cannot even condemn the transfiguration of his views by his self-appointed "apostles".

Paul is represented by Nietzsche as canonizing the errors of "the apostles" and thus erecting the first church wholly founded upon a mistake. Where Jesus starts with the refusal to make any concessions to rancor, Paul fashions Jesus into an instrument of revenge. The divine eschatology replaces the life of a spontaneous "yea-saying". The drama of redemptive history and the politics of salvation replace the life of individual bliss. The resurrection denies the very meaning of the crucifixion, saying yes even to death. Now one rushes head-long into the arms of the church to escape from death. The companion doctrine of original sin makes the past hang heavy like a dead weight aroung the neck. One runs head-long to the deadly doors of the church to escape the guillotine of existence.

The church announces the end of history. The redemptive eschatological drama unfolds: creation → fall → incarnation → crucifixion → resurrection → redemption. The church intends by the redemptive drama to accomplish the healing of the breach that defines man.

The God of the ancient Hebrews was praised by Nietzsche for strengthening the resolve of Israel, making the weak strong. Jesus, in seeking to arrest the declining will-to-power of the nation contemporary with his existence, steps outside of the historicity of Israel altogether.

Pauline Christianity sabotages Jesus's fundamental project by revaluing, out of 'ressentiment', the structures dominating the existence of an oppressed nation. The 'Genealogy of Morals', from which the following table is reconstructed, makes the significance of the revaluation clear:

I. Appearance of the Prevailing Structures	II. As Transvalued
1. Impotence, inability to retaliate	1. Goodness
2. Timorous lowliness	2. Humility

3. Submission towards those whom one hates	3. Obedience
4. "Obedience towards one whom they say deserves submission"	4. "God"
5. Cowardice, inoffensiveness of the weak	5. Patience, virtue
6. Inability to avenge	6. Voluntary renunciation of revenge; forgiveness.

The "other-worldliness" of Platonism was fashioned into an instrument of political revenge. Access to the "beyond" was to be gained through the transvaluation of the structures of 'eros' and *agon*:

"Here is sickness, beyond any doubt, the most terrible sickness that has ever raged in man; and whoever can still bear to hear (but today one no longer has ears for this!) how in this night of torment and absurdity there has resounded the cry of *love*, the cry of the most nostalgic rapture, of redemption through *love*, will turn away, seized by invincible horror. — There is so much in man that is hideous! — Too long, the earth has been a madhouse!"[212]

The West was only a few short steps away from nihilism.

d) The Path to Nihilism

Subsequently, philosophical activity is understood by Nietzsche as moving within the horizon of "Platonism" fused with Pauline Christianity. For Nietzsche, the history of philosophy represents a progressive falsification of the human spirit and, therefore, is understood as rendering man ever more remote from his true being.

In the 'Twilight of the Idols', Nietzsche presents a six-part epigram in which his analysis of the role of "reason in philosophy" culminates in a description of the history of metaphysics from out of 'ressentiment'. The epigram is entitled "How the 'True World' Finally Became a Fable". The subtitle of the epigram reveals the essence of the thematic characterization of the history of metaphysics as understood by Nietzsche: it is "The History of an Error". The error which propels the dialectical history of metaphysics, as understood by Nietzsche, is the progressive deprecation of the world of appearance and the corresponding promulgation of a fabricated substitute for appearance, i.e., "reality".

Immediately preceding the section on "How the 'True World' Finally Became a Fable", Nietzsche provides four propositions which are meant to inform the comprehension of his enigmatic presentation of the history of an error. The four propositions may be summarized as follows: 1) The world which appears and which we call "this world" is the only one because of the impossibility of demonstrating any other kind of reality; 2) The criteria for fabricating a "real world" antecedent to the apparent one are, in fact, criteria "constructed out of contradiction to the actual world"[213]; 3) The intending consciousness which generates a real world antecedent to the apparent one signifies the spirit of revenge against life itself; 4) To esteem a world beyond the apparent one, while deprecating the world of appearances, represents a recognition of the "decline of life". Against the conventional understanding of metaphysics which seeks to discover reality antecedent to appearance, Nietzsche affirms the value of appearance while bracketing the problem of "reality".

It is not clear that Nietzsche is himself either able or willing to ground the intelligibility of his four theses or his subsequent miniaturized six-part installment of the saga of the history of metaphysics. Yet, nowhere else in the corpus of his works does he present in so cogent, if compressed a form, his own version of the history of being.

The five stages Nietzsche characterizes in the "History of an Error" are: 1) Platonism — in which the world of becoming is knowingly and self-consciously deprecated and displaced by the world of Being; 2) Christianity — in which the metaphysics of Platonism represents Being as promised but unattainable in this world; 3) Kantianism — the union of sublimated Christianity and epistemological agnosticism: "The true world — unattainable, indemonstrable, unpromisable; but the very thought of it — consolation, an obligation, an imperative."[214] 4) The origin of positivism — Nietzsche characterizes this development as issuing from the aftermath of Kantianism and as a development of potentially liberating significance[215]: "The true world — unattainable? At any rate, unattained. And being unattained, also *unknown*. Consequently not consoling, redeeming, or obligating: How could something unknown obligate us? (Grey morning. The first yawn of reason. The cock-crow of positivism.)"[216]

If we take Nietzsche's previously characterized four propositions to heart, it is immediately evident that positivism rejects all attempts to substitute a substratum of "reality" either "beyond" or "behind" the world of appearances. Positivism rejects such investigation in explicit agreement with Nietzsche's first proposition as "absolutely indemonstrable"[217]. Moreover, while it performs a radical critique of pure reason, it rejects the burden of Kant's 'Critique of Practical Reason' as unsupportable because now all previously characterized "moral" utterances are understood as without cognitive significance.

The fifth and sixth stages of the history of Being, Nietzsche refrains from naming as such. However, it is evident that he has in mind the culmination of the previous four stages, i.e., the advent of the crisis of European Nihilism. In characterizing the fifth stage, that of the crisis of European Nihilism, Nietzsche celebrates its advent.

5): "The 'true' world — an idea which is no longer good for anything, not even obligating — an idea which has become useless and superfluous — *consequently*, a refuted idea: let us abolish it! (Bright day; breakfast; return of *bon sens* and cheerfulness; Plato's embarrassed blush; pandemonium of all free spirits.)"[218] Plato's "embarrassed blush" clearly refers back to the first stage and signifies that the Platonic falsification of becoming has become unmasked.

However, Nietzsche recognizes what the proponents of positivism fail to grasp — that it is now a time of 'pandemonium" for all free spirits. Why? The answer Nietzsche offers is in his characterization of the radical existential implications of the destruction of an illusion that has dominated and propelled the dialectic of Being from the time of Plato.

6): "The true world — we have abolished. What world has remained? The apparent one perhaps? But no! *With the true world, we have also abolished the apparent one.*"[219] Bernd Magnus graphically characterizes this devaluation of the apparent world.

"All that is left after the abolition of the true world is an aimless becoming in which all meaningful distinctions between veridical and delusory disappear. Indeed, the very possibility of meaningful criteriological distinctions becomes moot with the dissimulation of the 'true world'."[220]

Nietzsche characterizes this aimless relativity which he experienced in every sphere of reality — cultural, political, historical, and philosophical — as Nihilism. When the highest values become devalued, Nihilism emerges. But the highest values become de-valued not in the sense that man knowingly confronts an eternal abyss in fear and trembling. The highest values simply no longer exist. And man accepts this event not with stoic resignation but in total unawareness[221]. Nietzsche, however, is aware of the magnitude of this event and regards it as an opportunity to make a new beginning in comprehending the advent of European Nihilism as the prelude to the overcoming of the rancor against time and 'ressentiment' toward being. Subtending his characterization of the manifestation of European Nihilism, he remarks: "Noon, moment of the briefest shadow, end of the longest error; high point of humanity; INCIPIT ZARATHUSTRA."[222]

C. The Ontology of 'Ressentiment'

1. The Rancor Against Time

In a single remarkable epigram in 'Thus Spake Zarathustra' called "On Redemption", Nietzsche uncovers the metaphysical root of his reflection with these words spoken by Zarathustra:

"To redeem those who lived in the past and to recreate all 'it was' into a 'thus I willed it' — that alone should I call redemption. Will — that is the name of the liberator and joy-bringer; thus I taught you, my friends. But now learn this too: The will itself is still a prisoner. Willing liberates; but what is it that puts even the liberator himself in fetters? 'It was' — that is the name of the will's gnashing of teeth and most secret melancholy. Powerless against what has been done, he is an angry spectator of all that is past. The will cannot will backwards; and that he cannot break time and time's covetousness, that is the will's loneliest melancholy."[223]

Here, Nietzsche speaks of time as man stands related to it. There is no consideration of the nature of time apart from the way in which it appears to man and the impact which time is perceived by man as making on his life. Nietzsche emphasizes one phase of time, the "it was", as holding sway over human concerns. It is the past, the "it was" within time, that appears to occasion the grudge of man against time. How, and why, according to Nietzsche, is this the case?

Nietzsche's remarks about the past appear directed solely towards man's experience of the past. Experience of the past, even when characterized in a most insightful and disciplined manner, is not yet knowledge of the past. Still, Nietzsche speaks not merely of the past, but of the "It was" within time. This suggests that he is concerned with the being of the past, not simply with subjectively reported experiences of it.

In what manner can the past be said to have being when it is defined as that which is no longer capable of appearing except in the present? The past is that which was once possessed of being and is yet no longer. The past, it is implied by Nietzsche in the passage above, simply does not exist. Therefore, it would seem more correct, on Nietzsche's account, to call man's aversion to time his aversion to the past.

On this ontic level of analysis, Nietzsche's description of man's aversion to time, qualified as time past, appears paradoxical. Consider the statement: "Powerless against what has been done, he is an angry spectator of all that is past."[224] If we assume Nietzsche to mean that the past cannot be undone, we again presuppose a distinction which he himself does not make explicit between the deed of the past and the present interpretation of it. Yet, clearly, there are past deeds that are seen in a pleasant and favorable light when placed beneath the eye of memory, i.e., deeds that we should now, in the present, reckon as worthy; our recognition of them is accompanied by gladness rather than lamentation. Should Nietzsche, then, not confine man's complaint against the past to those deeds which he now, in the present, would rather have had or had been in some other way? Yet, if the "it was" within time is not possessed of being, the opposite should appear to be true. That is, genuine regret, remorse, self-recrimination are modes of self-deception. Because, when the past is understood as non-being there is no theater in which the drama of conscience can be performed.

Why, then, does Nietzsche say that "powerless against what has been done, man is an angry spectator of all that is past"? Should he rather have singled out those deeds deemed worthy in the present and now consigned to the oblivion of non-being? For here, human suffering can be sensed in the futility of all efforts to effect something of lasting or enduring value. The being of that which was once embraced in the full presence of appearance slips ineluctably beneath one's grasp and fades as surely as daylight is annihilated by evening.

The "it is" — the present, and the "it will be" — the future — still need to be reckoned with in terms of Nietzsche's understanding of man's rancor against time. Is a non-rancorous relation to time possible for the present and the future? Or, is rancor somehow at work in the perception of the present and the anticipation of the future? How can the spirit of revenge be said to belong to the whole of time when this judgment seems so plainly counter-intuitive? Are there not some occurrences to which everyone, some of the time, looks with expectant rejoicing. The presence that corresponds to the "it is" appears, at times, so over-full in the attractive and compelling looks of its appearance, as to make rancor towards it a departure from the overflowing and positive plurality of moods that dominate its appearance.

The future presents a peculiar metaphysical problem because human experience of that which will be and is not yet, appears logically impossible. For until the future is present, it is not. Given its non-existence, how can man in any sense be thwarted by it or experience rancor in relation to it? The apparent irreversibility of time which Nietzsche here presupposes should not cast a pall over that which still is or that which will be, seeing that neither the present nor the future have yet entered the train of fated irreversibility. This makes all the more enigmatic his remark:

"That time does not run backwards, that is his wrath; 'That which was' is the name of the stone he cannot move. And so he moves stones out of wrath and displeasure, and he wreaks revenge on whatever does not feel wrath and displeasure as he does. Thus the will, the liberator, took to hurting; and on all who can suffer, he wreaks revenge for his inability to go backwards. This, indeed, this alone is what *revenge* is: the will's ill will against time and its 'it was'."[225]

If the future and the present characterize those phases of time which yet live, the one in actuality, the other in prospect, why does Nietzsche link them to the train of fated irreversibility? Moreover, why does he appear to characterize the essence of the present especially, and the future with some more plausible cause, as though these phases of time were dominated by the non-reality which is thought to correspond to the 'it was?' And lastly, what is meant by the utterance that because 'that which was' "is the name of the stone he cannot move . . . he moves stones out of wrath and displeasure, and he wreaks revenge on whatever does not feel wrath and displeasure as he does?"

Nietzsche's reflection offered in "On Redemption" from 'Thus Spake Zarathustra' is his decisive variation on the theme considered in the earliest writings on Anaximander:

"Because there is suffering in those who will, inasmuch as they cannot will backwards, willing itself and all life were supposed to be — punishment. And now cloud upon cloud rolled over the spirit, until eventually madness preached: 'Everything passes away; therefore everything deserves to pass away. And this too is justice, this law of time that it must devour its children'. Thus preached madness."[226]

Now it is clear what Nietzsche means when he says that "Indeed, this alone is what *revenge* is: The will's ill will against time and its 'it was' ".

Everything that comes to be passes away. Every 'it is', every 'it will be' (after having become present and possessed of being) is destined to become 'it was'. In advance of its fleeting occurrence and temporary appropriation by Being, the ontological character of beings is that they are fated to a momentary rendezvous with Being before plunging into the vast, endless night of non-being. Here the distinction between the time of youth and the time of old-age collapses shipwrecked on the shoals of the rushing current of time without end, and an end without time.

The provisional characterization of the irreversibility of time may well, as Nietzsche asserts, dominate man's relation to the past and to the future, but it is not yet clear why the spirit of revenge should be said to dominate man's relation to the whole of time. The non-being of the past and of the future could provoke dread of that which is to come and resignation over that which is irremediably taken as completed and done. Why, then, has the spirit of revenge rather than dread, resignation, or even indifference "been the subject of man's best reflection"? Moreover, how does the desire for punishment arise out of the seemingly unconnected relation to time? Nietzsche's own resolution to these questions emerges with greater clarity when we retrieve consideration of the character and nature of the present — the 'it is' — which is presented by him as somehow buoying itself in the face of the ongoing storm of becoming that destroys the past and imperils the future.

The present, too, is fated to perish, to become the 'it was' within time. Yet, for the moment of its occurrence, it is possessed of duration. Always, the present emerges, manifests, and maintains itself prior to its perishing. Subsequently, Nietzsche will argue for a newly envisioned relation to time based upon his apprehension of the eternally reappearing presence of the 'it is'. However, such consideration of the doctrine of eternal return is premature until we understand more fully how it is that the present is understood by him as imprisoned within the train of the fated irreversibility of time.

The fact that Nietzsche offers his reflections on time in a fragmentary, episodic manner should not obscure the steely presentation of an idea methodically thought through and serving as a governing framework from out of which selected perspectives on the problem are presented. In the Prologue to 'Thus Spake Zarathustra', Zarathustra promises deliverance from the spirit of revenge.

"Man is a rope, tied between beast and over-man — a rope over an

abyss. A dangerous across, a dangerous on-the-way, a dangerous looking-back, a dangerous shuddering and stopping. What is great in man is
that he is a bridge and not an end: What can be loved in man is that he
is an *overture* and a *going under*. ... I love him who casts golden
words before his deeds and always does even more than he promises:
For he wants to go under. I love him who justifies future and redeems
past generations: For he wants to perish of the present."[227]

The key to Zarathustra's keeping of his promise to prepare the
way for the "supra-man" is Nietzsche's own capacity to reckon successfully with the spirit of revenge. The Prologue introducing 'Thus Spake
Zarathustra' advances the notion that man as formed and to-date is,
himself, a prologue, a bridge, an overture, to what he is to become.

In the face of man's obsession with time's passing, his preoccupation has been, according to Nietzsche, to advance out of the spirit of
revenge, a self-definition that deprives him of the recognition of the
promissory character of his own being. On his way only towards the
nothingness harbored within the shadow of the 'it was' within time,
the identity of being human manifests itself emphatically, essentially,
and exclusively against that which is *not-beast*. The Aristotelian
concept of man as *zoon logikon echon* is interpreted by Nietzsche as
an expression of the rancor against time.

Heidegger's profound and original recasting of Nietzsche's thought
on the revenge against time makes this point evident. Enigmatically
entitled 'What Is Called Thinking?', Heidegger's meditation on Nietzsche's doctrine of deliverance from revenge is prefaced by an apparently unrelated concern that summons man to think about the nature of
thinking: *"Most thought-provoking is that we are still not thinking —*
not even yet, although the state of the world is becoming constantly
more thought-provoking."[228] Corresponding to what is, and has been
called thinking, is the understanding of the being of thinking decisively formed for occidental metaphysics in the thought of Aristotle. Expressive of the *energeia* of man is the life of active *nous*. Active *nous*
is arrested in the moment of its triumph, i.e., when *nous* is possessed
by that which no longer moves. It is in this moment that man becomes thoughtfulness itself and lives wholly in the deathless grasp of
the eternal "Now". Perfect thoughfulness is that which no longer becomes, for it has arrived at its appointed end. The appointed end of
thoughtfulness is the perfect union of knower and known. The simultaneous and reciprocal appropriation of being and knowing crosses
the threshhold from time to eternity. Unity against self-dispersion is

achieved by placing man beyond the upsurging ravages waiting at the entrance and exit of the portals to eternity, the 'it was' and the 'it will be' within time. Hence, what has been called "thinking" represents a flight from the temporal character of human existence. Implicit in this flight is a submerged anger against that which appears to mandate its necessity, human transience.

Nothing less than a radical transformation of human passion and longing in relation to time can transform that which "has been called thinking" into thinking, with its forward thrust beyond the spirit of revenge against time. For Nietzsche, this demands envisioning a new relatedness on the part of man to the being of the "it is" within time. This means that he must at once be prepared to let go of his grudge against the impacting presence of the 'it was' character that belongs to time's appropriation of the whole of man's being. The alarming character of the present which causes man to cling to it as though a life raft in the turbulent ocean of terrifying possibility, is the recognition of its finality. It is not simply a dread of losing being to the 'it was' within time, but the simultaneous recognition that that which is now present is destined to become past — that is fixed, immovable, and true for all time — that occasions the incursion of the spirit of revenge into the present moment.

Ontological falsification begins when the spirit of revenge is directed against the source and ground from out of which all appearances of human suffering emerge; time's passing. *Nietzsche's thesis affirms that man suffers not in time but from time*. Harking back to the early reflection on Anaximander, he has Zarathustra remark: "No deed can be annihilated: how could it be undone by punishment? This, this is what is eternal in the punishment called existence, that existence must eternally become deed and guilt again."[229] The arrangement of time is such, Nietzsche implies, as to require of every present moment that it is fated to become incomplete and imperfect as it yields to its permanent character, i.e., the "it was" within time. Hence arises the existential guilt that derives from the absence of completeness in which each deed is enveloped, and the companion demand for finality that must always fail of being met. Rather than striving for the release from the spirit of revenge occasioned by time's passing, *man strives for release from time*.

The spirit of revenge born from the rancor against time's passing is subjected to the work of 'ressentiment' in the moment when earthly time is devalued as that "which merely passes", as that "which is merely transitory". Yet, it is human existence which has been understood from the time of Anaximander, from out of the spirit of revenge, as the ultimate accident that befalls man, and, therefore, as unjustifiable and reckoned as deserving of punishment. Through the falsified projection of "eternity" reckoned out of the spirit of revenge, the accident of temporal, human existence is inflicted. Time's passing has become for occidental metaphysics (and so for every man in the West) that which is inessential, that which is merely transitory. Eternity mocks the aspirations of those who would establish the stamp of permanence upon all deeds, by invalidating in advance the deed of existence.

The time of eternity, as reckoned out of the spirit of revenge, is an infinite series of unchanging "nows"[230]. Therefore, the changeless character of eternity is fashioned as an avenging angel that wreaks vengeance upon all temporal existence in which the "now" that appears is destined to become the "it was". Ergo, the Platonic contemplation of the deathless and unchanging *eide*; the beyond of Pauline Christianity; the indemonstrable and, therefore, consoling noumenal realm of Kant, and now, in the deepest night of Nihilism, only suffering, guilt, and the spirit of revenge.

Existential suffering reflects the awareness of abandonment. When "the cockcrow of positivism" has shorn the world of Aristotle's final causality, and heralded the death of the redemptive power of the God above gods there is only human truth, the truth of transience. The end of life signifies the death of meaning. Man recognizes himself as finite but, in failed expectation of a transfinite longing, cannot reach an accomodation with the way things are. All that is true is what appears. Therefore all that matters is determined in the present hour when Being manifests itself. How can we be expected to let go of our grasp of the present hour knowing that it is destined to become truth and yet human truth — therefore, destined to imperfection and error. For there is no residuum of promise, on Nietzsche's account, in the "it was" within time.

Existential guilt begins in this recognition of the fated finality of the present. Each present hour must appear in full dress — for there is no time for self-rehearsals or for the provisional, only the fatedness of error. That which is met with as the present must be completed and perfected before we let it go to the past — to truth. For the past is the mirror in which is reflected the errors of the present. What is present shall become past, and the past shall make its way into the coming present such that we shall be bound and unfree in the face of the hour that arrives. It is in the reflection of this mirror, of the 'it was' within time, that man sees himself as "a dangerous looking-back, a dangerous shuddering and stopping" without sensing — because of the spirit of revenge — that he is also "a bridge and not an end".

The last and most radical expression of the 'ressentiment'-devaluation of time, on Nietzsche's view, is a turning against the fundamental thrust of being human — willing itself: " 'Unless the will should at last redeem himself, and willing should become not willing'. But, my brothers, you know this fable of madness."[231] For, in Nietzsche's view, it is through the phenomenon of the will reconceived as the ultimate and self-defining act of all beings to maintain, assert, and thereby manifest themselves that the nothingness of Being is defied. This ontological striving which Nietzsche calls the "will-to-power" aims at no end, and can aim to no end, other than that of the radical act of self-assertion whereby beings manifest themselves through the striving to become, through the striving that holds out against the ontological ground of all nothingness. When Nietzsche speaks of the madness of the desire for release from the will-to-power, he signifies the inseparable ontological interdependency of suffering, striving, time, existence, and philosophy.

The recognition of this interlocking set of meanings dates back to Plato's 'Symposium'. In the 'Symposium', philosophy is defined by Socrates as the yearning after wisdom, the desire to be or know that which one either is not or knows not. Nietzsche's concept of the will-to-power corresponds in several of its essential respects to 'eros', as conceived by the Platonic Socrates. Platonic 'eros' represents the forward thrust of man without which he could not be summoned forth by that which appears in the guise of the beautiful, the true, and the good. Nietzsche's doctrine of the will-to-power is, like Platonic 'eros', not reckoned as an exclusively connative faculty of man. It is not understood as a faculty that inheres within the human *psyche*. 'Eros' has the power to bind man to being, and, as such, reflects the capacity to take on a cognitive significance. Man can only know that which he has an affinity for being drawn towards. Otherwise, we should not be able to explain the selectivity of perception upon which reflection depends for its content.

For Nietzsche, as for Plato's 'eros', the will-to-power demands that which it lacks, and therefore suffers from. That which claims the will-to-power attracts it by acting as a beacon towards which it gravitates. Lastly, and decisively, human existence aims at crossing the

threshold of mortality — for that is what 'eros' — always striving, always yearning, always reaching towards — most essentially lacks.
However, while Plato confines the activity of 'eros' to beings capable
of assuming a non-reducible biological character, Nietzsche asserts that
the will-to-power essentially pertains to, appropriates, and in that
sense, bestows the character of existence on all beings[232].

Moreover, Nietzsche emphatically denies what Plato asserts in
regard to the ontological ground which summons forth the cognitive,
connative, and appetitive striving of man — the Good transcendent to
Being, knowing, and willing. Authentic philosophy depends, for
Plato, upon both the reality of the Good and the capacity to transform the striving of 'eros' towards that which is stamped with the
character of being good, as measured against the criterion of its not
being susceptible to the corruption of time.

Nietzsche rejects, with Plato and against Schopenhauer (and the
spirit of the East), the temptation to rid man of suffering by having
the will-to-power abandon its own self-defining forward thrusting. The
will-to-power turned inward against itself, in the project of seeking
its own abandonment, can rid man of suffering only by giving up on,
and in that sense denying, time, existence, and the mortality that
recognizes itself in the aspiration to cross its own self-defining limit.
"But, my brothers, you know this fable of madness." Previously, the
will-to-power preserved itself by contrasting and inverting its inten-
al thrust. The Socratic and Christian transvaluation of values served
for Nietzsche, as we have seen, as decisive turnings in the subterranean
history of the will-to-power. The 'ressentiment' governing the devaluation of the will-to-power employs a new and more radical strategy to
alleviate human suffering than any that has come before. False and
consoling modes of self-transcendence are no longer viable, historicity is to be left undisturbed, but now in a consummate act of 'ressentiment', to be deprived of its meaning. It is the time of the last man,
the man who devalues the promise of authentic self-transcendence
that is at hand:

"Alas, the time is coming when man will no longer give birth to a star.
Alas, the time of the most despicable man is coming, he that is no
longer able to despise himself. Behold, I show you the *last man*.
'What is love? What is creation? What is longing? What is a star?' Thus
asks the last man, and he blinks. The earth has become small, and on
it hops the last man, who makes everything small. His race is as

ineradicable as the flea-beetle; the last man lives longest. 'We have invented happiness', say the last men."[233]

The last man invents a happiness derived from small pleasures not born of the spirit of longing. For longing brings suffering. Suffering reflects the passion of self-assertion in the face of time's passing. Self-assertion in the face of time's passing mandates the forward and outward thrust of the will-to-power in the face of transience. But the will-to-power has disfigured itself in the last man who longs for nothing so as to escape his suffering. The last man disputes the reality of love, creation, and longing because he lacks the will-to-power requisite for all orientation towards that (star) that lies beyond man and summons forth the spirit of creation. The last man blinks from the embarrassing recognition that in turning against the will-to-power, he is contracting his vision perpetually and, thus, dispossessing himself of an outlook and an orientation towards that which arrests the reflective gaze of the mind's eye.

Governed by the spirit of revenge the will-to-power of the "last man" turns against itself and, in this dynamic inversion, supplants honor with humility and shame with pity. 'Ressentiment'-humility is the spirit of pity directed against the self, which by inverting the will-to-power, seeks to sustain the self: "When stepped on, a worm doubles up. That is clever. In that way he lessens the probability of being stepped on again. In the language of morality: humility."[234] Like the worm, the "last man" wishes to secure a modest outpost in Being without manifesting the will-to-become, and thus risks the attendant consequences. In "On the Pitying" from "Thus Spake Zarathustra", Nietzsche explains. "To him who has knowledge, man himself is 'the animal with red cheeks'. How did this come about?"
"Is it not because man has had to be ashamed too often? . . . Thus speaks he who has knowledge: Shame, shame, shame — that is the history of man. And that is why he who is noble bids himself not to shame: Shame he imposes on himself before all who suffer. Verily, I do not like them, the merciful who feel blessed in their pity: they are lacking too much in shame. If I must pity, at least I do not want it known; and if I do pity, it is preferably from a distance."[235]

Unable to comport itself with honor, the will-to-honor hides itself from the inseparable companion of honor, i.e., shame. Out of the spirit of revenge, unable to maintain itself against the absence of honor, springs an unwillingness to live with the presence of shame. To reckon with the strength attendant on the will-to-honor, one must be willing to live in the atmosphere of present shame or turn against the claiming reality of the previously esteemed excellence of honor. To pity, for Nietzsche, means to give up on the presence of shame and the claiming power of absent honor.

Mere self-maintenance is, as understood by Nietzsche, comprehensible only within the horizon of the forward and outward thrusting of the will-to-power. Self-preservation taken as the end of human striving is comprehended dialectically, by Nietzsche, as a fatedness to 'ressentiment'. The ontological inversion characteristic of 'ressentiment'-laden valuation of the will-to-power permits man to abide in the meanwhile of Being; but this self-abiding is understood as decline and decay in the absence of an horizon opening on to self-transformation. It harbors its greater danger when it becomes forgetful of what it is — a sublimated abiding and holding out that becomes mistaken for the truth of the will-to-power.

What holds sway in the political, cultural, and religious institutions of the day is already on its way towards a decision of what is to become of man. The last man is he who no longer recognizes that his 'ressentiment' is a retreat and retrenchment, however necessary, in the face of the onslaught of forces that can no longer be faced directly. The "last man" gives up the promise of man in shrinking from the will-to-become himself through time; he gives up on history.

Through the personage of Zarathustra, Nietzsche sees himself as preparing the way for the overcoming of the last man. The function of Zarathustra is to act as a bridge between the realigned possibilities antecedent to the existence of the last man and the fashioning of the image of man-to-come, the "supra-man". Zarathustra promises the advent of the "supra-man" by divesting the will-to-power of the spirit of revenge. This means that Zarathustra must teach liberation from the rancor against time and the subsequent devaluation of the will-to-power from out of which issues the 'ressentiment' against Being.

"The now and the past on earth . . . is what *I* find most unendurable; and I should not know how to live if I were not also a seer of that which must come. A seer, a willer, a creator, a future himself, and a bridge to the future — and, alas, also, as it were, a cripple at this bridge: all this is Zarathustra."[236]

Zarathustra is a bridge to the future, even a "cripple at this bridge", just because he is handicapped by the spirit of revenge which informs, with obdurate power, the last man whose very spirit must be overcome. He is able to refrain from blinking and to envisage what must come if the last men are to be overcome. In that sense, he is a "bridge" because he is man on the way to becoming "supra-man".

Zarathustra promises the future of man to man. How, according to Nietzsche, does Zarathustra propose to make good on this promise: "I walk among men as among the fragments of the future — the future which I envisage. And this is all my creating and striving, that I create and carry together into One what is fragment and riddle and dreadful accident. And how could I bear to be a man if man were not also a creator and guesser of riddles and redeemer of accidents."[237]

The fragments of the future are to be fashioned from out of the realigned possibilities dormant in the present. The accident of which Zarathustra speaks is existence. It must be revalued as a blessing rather than a curse. The 'ressentiment' against becoming is responsible for interpreting existence as a curse. To eliminate the "beyond" of time without succumbing to a devaluation of the will-to-power is to permit man to go beyond himself as fashioned to-date: "For *that man be delivered from revenge*, that is for me the bridge to the highest hope, and a rainbow after long storms."[238]

2. The Doctrine of Eternal Return

Zarathustra is the bridge to the highest hope. The path he opens leads to a rainbow after long storms. Zarathustra teaches the doctrine of eternal return that overcomes the 'ressentiment' of the last man and, therefore, engenders the possibility of the "supra-man". Nietzsche leaves no doubt as to Zarathustra's function. Looking back on his writings in 'Ecce Homo', Nietzsche says about 'Thus Spake Zarathustra': "The fundamental conception of this work, the idea of eternal recurrence, this highest formula of affirmation of all that is attainable, belongs in August 1881: It was penned on a sheet with the notation underneath, 'Six thousand feet beyond man and time'."[239]

The animals of Zarathustra, the eagle and the serpent, "the proudest animal under the sun and the wisest animal under the sun" declare the teaching of Zarathustra: "Behold, *you are the teacher of the eternal recurrence* — that is your destiny! ... Behold, we know what you teach: that all things recur eternally, and we ourselves too; and that we have already existed an eternal number of times, and all things with us. You teach that there is a great year of becoming, a monster of a great year, which must, like an hourglass, turn over again and again so that it may run down and run out again; and all these years are alike in what is greatest as in what is smallest; and we ourselves are alike in every great year, in what is greatest as in what is smallest."[240]

In the 'Will To Power' the thesis of the eternal recurrence is advanced in a formula: "To impose upon becoming the character of being — that is the supreme will-to-power . . . That *everything recurs* is the closest *approximation of a world of becoming to a world of being*: — high point of the meditation."[241]

Everything that comes to be is destined to pass away — and, it is destined to do so eternally. Every "it is" within time is destined to reappear exactly as it once did. The lost "presence" of the present is preserved not in recollection or anticipation, but, it is asserted, in its virtual reappearances. In "On the Vision and the Riddle", Zarathustra throws open the gateway locking in the rancor against time:

"Behold this gateway, dwarf! . . . It has two faces. Two paths meet here; no one has yet followed either to its end. This long lane stretches back for an eternity. And the long lane out there, that is another eternity. They contradict each other, these paths; they offend each other face to face; and it is here at this gateway that they come together. The name of the gateway is inscribed above: 'Moment.' But who ever would follow one of them, on and on, farther and farther — do you believe, dwarf, that these paths contradict each other eternally?

'All that is straight lies', the dwarf murmured contemptuously. 'All truth is crooked, time itself is a circle'."[242]

The moment as characterized by Zarathustra is conceived as the ever-recurring "it is" within time. What is now, the presence of the now, is preserved from eternal destruction because it will come again, and forever.

The next passage from the section entitled "On the Vision and the Riddle" universalizes the assertion that what is now, must have already been exactly as it now is in a time past: "And if everything has been there before . . . must not this gateway (this moment) have been there before? And are not all things knotted together so firmly that this moment draws after it *all* that is to come? Therefore — itself too?"[243] Every moment, therefore, adumbrates a two-fold eternity, an eternity of times it has already been, an eternity of times that are to come.

Nietzsche does not clarify the question of what is to constitute a moment. The assumption that governs the subsequent description of configurations of beings and events that are said to eternally recur, is that the moment is not indefinitely divisible. Whatever else it is, it must be of sufficient duration such that recognizable forms, figures, and events can manifest themselves long enough for Zarathustra to describe their appearances. "And this slow spider, which crawls in the moonlight, and this moonlight itself, and I and you in the gateway, whispering together, whispering of eternal things — must not all of us have been there before? And return and walk in that other lane . . . — must we not eternally return?"[244] Each moment, however possessed of duration, is fated to take its place as the "it was" within the fated irreversibility of time. It is destined to come again.

The doctrine of eternal return is philosophically provocative and ambiguous. Will the moment come again because we so desire it, or do we desire it because it will come again? The thesis of eternal return by itself affirms that the moment will actually recur, and that is why we should desire it. However, the inseparable companion of the thesis of eternal return is the concept of the "supra-man"[245]. The "supra-man" is the being who desires, and therefore wills, that the moment recur eternally.

For Nietzsche the two-fold doctrine of eternal return and the "supra-man" are inseparable from his reflection on nihilism. Taking them together as two aspects of the eternal return, Nietzsche intends to accomplish nothing less than the revaluation of all values.

It is not by accident that the doctrine of eternal return precisely transforms the essence of nihilism. Immediately preceding the epigram "On Redemption", Zarathustra encapsulates the essence of nihilism in a formula: ". . . And I saw a great sadness descend upon mankind. The best grew weary of their works. A doctrine appeared, accompanied by a faith: 'All is empty, all is the same, all has been!' "[246] The structural positioning of the section on "The Soothsayer", from which the passage above is cited, and the epigram "On Redemption" parallels, in a striking manner, the dialectical stages of the history of metaphysics as expressed by Nietzsche in the 'Twilight of the Idols'. The doctrine of eternal return sets out to revalue the essence of nihilism. 'All is full, all is the same, all will come again'.

The dialectical revaluation is not won merely in the realm of speech. The development of nihilism provides the indispensable ontological condition for the capacity to reckon with the meanings or essences of beings. Only when it can clearly be seen that each being exists for no greater end than itself, can the *existentia* of all beings, the eternal return, be made manifest. Reflecting on the formula of nihilism, Zarathustra says: "Verily, we have become too weary even to die."[247] To die, means that the *essentia* of the will-to-exist eternally, must become manifest and, in turn, manifest becoming.

It is by dramatic design, then, that the section on "The Soothsayer" precedes the shattering speech poured forth in the epigram "On Redemption". The premise of the doctrine of eternal return emerges out of dialectical struggle with the conclusion that characterizes the essence of nihilism. Drama again serves to intensify concept, when Nietzsche, in the secton "On the Convalescent", has Zarathustra withdraw into a bottomless solitude prior to an ecstatic rapture in which the doctrine of eternal return is described.

For seven days Zarathustra refuses to eat or drink, and most uncharacteristically, to speak. Zarathustra has been overcome by a profound nausea, the nausea that accompanies the sickness of nihilism. There is only the accident of existence and the eternal suffering to which it is fated. 'All is empty, all is the same.' There is no reason for anything at all to be; it merely is. It is destined to come again just as it has been, without reason or purpose or foundation. There is only the ever recurring rancor against time and the metaphysical circle of 'ressentiment': "Zarathustra, the godless, summons you! I, Zarathustra, the advocate of life, the advocate of suffering, the advocate of the circle; I summon you, my most abysmal thought."[248]

The remedy, the rapture borne of the eternal return is pregnant in the nausea of nihilism: "Hail to me! You are coming, I hear you. My abyss speaks, I have turned to ultimate depth inside out into the light. Hail to me! Come here! Give me your hand! Huh! Let go! Huhhuh! Nausea, nausea, nausea — woe unto me!"[249]

After having languished for seven days Zarathustra is summoned out of his slumber. The symbolism is heavy-handed and unmistakable: "At last, after seven days, Zarathustra raised himself on his resting place, took a rose apple into his hand, smelled it, and found its fragrance lovely. Then his animals thought that the time had come to speak with him.

'O Zarathustra', they said, 'it is now seven days that you have been lying like this with heavy eyes; won't you at last get up on your feet again? Step out of your cave: the world awaits you like a garden ... All things have been longing for seven days. Step out of your cave! All things would be your physicians. Has perhaps some new

knowledge came to you, bitter and hard? Like leavened dough you
you have been lying; your soul rose and swelled over its rims."[250]

A new man is being created out of nothingness. The time of his
gestation is seven days. The extra day is needed because he is to be
more complete than his precursor. His longing for eternity is to be
sated in time. He eats the fruit of wisdom, and it returns him to a
garden of primal innocence, richer than the first. The serpent of
wisdom beckons him home to eternity, not astray into history and
exile.

Zarathustra confirms his new "knowledge" with the soaring pride
of an eagle, not with abject shame or humility. Nausea, the global
response of disgust at the gratuitousness of beings, gives way to
rejoicing, to the gratitude that they should be as they are.

Zarathustra teaches the revaluation of the meaning of speech.
Language explains nothing, justifies nothing. It exists so that man
might bless the things that are, so that he might rejoice over creation,
his creation.

"Have not names and sounds been given to things so that man might
find things refreshing? Speaking is a beautiful folly: with that man
dances over all things. How lovely is all talking, and all the deception
of sounds. With sounds our love dances on many-hued rainbows."[251]

The power of naming belongs to Zarathustra, as to a god. Speech
communicates nothing but the will-to-command. It is not purposeful
but expressional, born out of overfullness.

Zarathustra penetrates the theodicy of grammar: "'Reason' in
language — oh, what an old deceptive female she is! I am afraid we are
not rid of God because we still have faith in grammar?"[252] The demand for reasons betrays an ontological category mistake. 'There is
no outside-myself.' How could there be, when there is no outside, no
ground of existence ulterior to the sheer facticity of becoming. Every
utterance veils an existential assertion. That assertion presumes that
anything can be explained or justified, which is always to say the same
thing. It is to commit the fallacy of Anaximander, to believe that
there is a logic exterior to the reality of transience, or the fiat of the
will.

It is not the limits of language that pre-ordain the limits of understanding the world. It is rather the world that withholds from speech
that which it has not the power to give.

Speech is adequate to express the way things are. In an ecstatic

outpouring the animals of Zarathustra respond to his reflections on language by celebrating the doctrine of eternal recurrence of same;
" 'O Zarathustra', the animals said, 'To those who think as we do, all things themselves are dancing: They come and offer their hands and laugh and flee — and come back. Everything goes, everything comes back; eternally rolls the wheel of being, everything dies, everything blossoms again; eternally runs the year of being. Everything breaks, everything is joined anew; eternally the same house of being is built. Everything parts, everything greets every other thing again; eternally the ring of being remains faithful to itself. In every Now, being begins; round every Here rolls the sphere There. The center is everywhere. Bent is the path of eternity."[260]

The doctrine of eternal return seeks to redefine man as the being who esteems the essential character of coming-to-be. How, though, does the doctrine of eternal return function to liberate man from the rancor against time?

Zarathustra imposes the task for that which is "over-man". Every "it is", the momentary "now", shall be made subject to the criterion that it be momentous. The meaning and value of every "it is" shall be judged by the criterion that we shall long to have it return. Submission without rancor to the ordinance of time is possible because transience is freed from its pathos. The will-to-power in regard to the moment is accompanied by a will to let the moment perish. The rendezvous with the next moment no longer need be spent digesting overlong that which is now no longer, because it will come again.

All that comes to be is to be estimated, in the light of the perpetual regard which he will have, of its having come-to-be. Since man gives the gift of becoming to himself, he stands in the debt of no one but himself. Therefore, according to Nietzsche's reckoning, the doctrine of eternal return serves to rid man of the existential guilt that derives from the falsified notion that man is indebted to Being for the arrangement of time.

Every moment reconceived under the aegis of eternal return has a consummatory character. It is destined to take its place in the ever-recurring cycle of becoming and is, therefore, to be regarded as possessed of a momentous quality. The doctrine of eternal return is intended to liberate man from his falsified attachments to all things beyond the horizon of his rendezvous with the moment, and, therefore, to rid him once and for all of the 'ressentiment' against becoming.

Zarathustra promises the coming of the overman, the being who will gladly yoke himself to the doctrine of eternal return. The over-man is "the animal *with the right to make promises*", the solution to "the paradoxical task that nature has set itself in the case of man . . . the real problem regarding man"[254].

What he now is, he must be prepared to will again. In the face of everything that is chance and accident, he will interpose necessity without recourse to or reliance upon external authority. When he lets go his word into the indeterminate, but fated future, there, too, he will go in the shape of the self-defining deed of his own becoming. The ultimate accident, existence itself, he will redeem by transforming chance into necessity through the will-to-power. History is to become the subject of his intention and the expression of his power; and therefore, while still fated, no longer begrudged. For the "supra-man" is to will time's passing in advance and ahead of time's advent. Word and deed are to be wedded into an indissoluble unity which in turn binds together past and future with the present. The "supra-man" will be a joy-bringer as well as a liberator. The spirit of revenge will give way to a cosmic enthusiasm in which man will gladly and know-ingly permit himself to be possessed by the moment and become that which passes and is destined to return. The decadence of the spiritual life of western man will move to a new key of self-ascendance, that is irreversible with a transvaluation of things earthly. Just as the rancor against time will be supplanted for an enthusiasm of the moment, so too will the 'ressentiment' against being yield to a rightful esteem for that which is on its way, i.e., that which becomes.

Nietzsche offers concrete intimations of that which is "overman" and towards which man will move when the rancor against time is overcome. The meaning of 'eros' will be transformed. A man will wish to beget progeny, not to break the bounds of his mortality, but rather to affirm his immortality[255]. The eternal recurrence of same has al-ready insured his perpetual possession of 'the good'.

The meaning of *agon* will be revalued. The struggle for honor and recognition will be transformed to a plane that is titanic and trans-historical:
"How divinely vault and arches break through each other in a wrestl-ing match; how they strive against each other with light and shade, the godlike strivers — with such assurance and beauty let us be enemies too, my friends! Le us strive against one another like gods!"[256]

With the transvaluation of *agon*, the meaning of *philia* is revalued. One cannot take up the stance of 'agape', as a god towards a mortal, without devaluing in advance the godlike striving of the other. For "to every soul there belongs another world; for every soul, every other soul is an afterworld"[257]. It is not the loving of the enemy, as well as the friend, that Zarathustra teaches as the way to the overman; it is rather honoring the enemy *in* the friend, and the enmity and danger one harbors within oneself for the friend:

"If one wants to have a friend one must also want to wage war for him: and to wage war, one must be *capable* of being an enemy. . . . In a friend one should have one's best enemy. You should be closer to him with your heart when you resist him."[258]

Out of the darkest night of Nihilism, where God is presumed dead, the dawn of man as god has broken through distant clouds. The doctrine of the "supra-man" affirms a single thesis: Man is a great god, and his will is supreme. The questioning of what it means to be divine and what it means to be human can now, for the first time, be understood as one question to which only man himself can give the answer. To be divine means to command, to legislate, to make meaningful, to promise and to act as the guarantor of that which one promises. It means to forge order out of chaos, promise out of nothingness, an eternity out of time. It means to affirm all contingencies in advance of their happening and to celebrate the divine project of creation.

The revolutionary character of the revaluation of the meaning of all beings as reflections of the will-to-power consists in the making explicit of that which has remained concealed in the history of western philosophy from its conception. The development of Nihilism to its most radical appearance provides the indispensable ontological condition for the capacity to reckon with the meanings or essences of beings. For, only when it can be clearly seen that each being exists for the sake of no end greater than itself and the manifestation of its will-to-power, can the *essentia* of that which is common to all beings itself be made manifest.

The revaluation of the meaning of beings occasioned by the ontological ground of nothingness permits a reconceiving of how it stands with Being such that beings can be invested with meaning. The *existentia* belonging to every being is to recur eternally. The doctrine of eternal return, Nietzsche believes, at last frees the drama of coming-to-be of a falsified and superimposed cosmodicy. Time is not a slippage from the wheel of eternity, nor a fall from divine to terrestrial habitation. Time is not "the moving image of eternity" but the many and recurring expressions on the face of eternity itself.

D. Criticism and Conclusion

1. Criticism

There is an emphatic difference between the assertions of a philosopher and the capacity of a philosopher to withstand sustained criticisms of his founding assumptions. Nietzsche's insistence on the virtual non-existence of the past and the future demonstrates that the doctrine of eternal return is unable to metaphysically ground the deliverance of man from the spirit of revenge. As a resolution to the rancor against time, the theory of eternal return suffers from the following defects:

First, from a narrowly conceived, logical point of view, there must either be a divisibility to the *Moment* or a bifurcation in consciousness that permits us to recollect that in the *same* Moment, the Moment will come again. Nietzsche does not demonstrate how it is possible to fully engage the Moment while remembering that our very act of recollection — if it is within time — cannot but detract from our abandonment to it.

Secondly, the ever recurring "it is" within time is insufficient to ontologically ground the instrumental and consummatory phases of experienced time. It is, therefore, inconceivable that "supra-man" could promise anything at all, since the moments of the making and keeping of a promise would necessarily be coincident. The concept of promising would, thereby, be rendered incomprehensible.

In the third place, it is unclear how Nietzsche's theory of time, reconceived under the aegis of the doctrine of eternal return, permits a philosophically comprehensible account of the claims of mathematics and science, order and justice, rest and stability. The *eternity* of each "now" is purchased at the price of its being self-contained and, therefore, eternally unrelated to every other "now".

In the fourth place, Nietzsche's doctrine of the eternal return of *same*, raises the question of how any being can be self-same, such that it could once be said to have appeared as *one*. The recurrence of beings, no matter how many times repeated will never yield unity when the single manifestation of unity is denied its possibility. The doctrine of eternal recurrence of same mistakenly seeks to ground the possible appearance of unity out of an indefinite number of recurring expressions of manyness.

Most paradoxically, and in the fifth place, it is philosophically incomprehensible how anything at all can meaningfully be said to *become*, let alone recur, under the doctrine of eternal recurrence of same.

We might reasonably ask how a calendar is possible from the stand-point of eternal return? How are years, or days, or hours to be fash-ioned out of moments that have no apparent duration or internal relation to each other?

Nietzsche's thought of eternal return does not seek refuge from logical contradictions, epistemological paradoxes, and metaphysical tangles. To Heraclitus, Nietzsche nods in apparent agreement that "it is impossible to step twice into the same river"[259]. The position advanced by the student of Heraclitus, who said that it "is impossible to step into the same river once", seems even more representative of Nietzsche. Nietzsche must either assent or remain silent when it is pointed out that to speak of any river at all from his perspective is impossible. It is an instance of the inability to ground the reality of all nouns since there are no stable objects to which they could refer.

The doctrine of eternal return affirms, then, the dazzling contra-diction that: 1) Man cannot step into the same river once because to do so would imply that the everflowing river stopped for even a moment; 2) Man cannot step outside of the river even once because to do so would assume that all of the instances of time do not mani-fest themselves simultaneously in the Moment. Therefore, 3) everyone both does and does not step into the same river twice, at all times, in the same respect. Lastly 4) everyone shall go on both stepping and not stepping into the same river without end as they have already done innumerable times before.

2. Conclusion

Nietzsche's radical historicism culminates in affirming the end, not of philosophy or metaphysics, but of history. Deliverance, from the spirit of revenge conceives of the concept of history as itself resulting from 'ressentiment'. The imposition of an artificial drama upon the sensory tangle of transience is the falsification stemming from 'ressentiment' that Nietzsche locates as governing the fiction of human history, for it invests the "beyond" with the possibility of engendering purposive-ness and orientation which belie the facts, as he says, they disclose themselves. In denying the reality of history Nietzsche closes man off from an openness to the possibility of reconceiving metaphysics. The virtual nonexistence of the future and the past means that man can be informed only by the ever recurring momentary appearance of the "it is" within time. Time so conceived is not a gateway to metaphysics reconceived; rather, it is the gate that closes on existence as well as thought. Hence, the claim that with Nietzsche, metaphysics has come full circle leaving only the abysmal thought of Anaximander, shorn of promise as well as 'ressentiment', as the only true report on the way man stands with Being.

The enduring strength of Nietzsche's analysis of the rancor against time lies in the way it manages to render explicit the decision that confronts man when the rancor against time has been disclosed. The way which Nietzsche wished to open to man would, in the words of Tillich, be one where "self-affirmation is the affirmation of life and of the death which belongs to life"[260].

Nietzsche's failure to validate his rich abundance of insights and to ground his exhortation stems from an inner allegiance to the ruling state of affairs anchoring the western philosophic tradition. He remains claimed by a theory of Being, of man, of time, and of the world that ends in turning his own most profound insight against the intentions of the author[261].

The doctrine of eternal return sets out to reconcile man with the death of meaning by revaluing life as deathless and time as endless. The inseparable companion doctrine of the "overman" sought to redefine the being of man such that he might manifest himself with an ontological integrity and primacy in relation to himself and all other beings. The concept of the "overman" ended in affirming that man is a great god, who through the agency of his supreme will, is prepared to rule over a world that he remakes at each of the recurring intervals of time without end. In absolute contradiction to his expressed intention, Nietzsche's two-fold doctrine of eternal return and the overman taken together, revalues the meaning of Being as a deathless "beyond", the unfolding of time as an ever recurring series of discrete eternities, and places an omnipotent and omniscient god in the midst of the revalued world.

It is a world which has no need or possibility of philosophy, defined either as the love of wisdom or the science and practice of wisdom. The will-to-power reigns unchecked and without limit. In advance, its shadow falls upon and invalidates the activity of interpretation as a derpived mode of essential self-expression. The revaluation of man as the animal possessed by thought is incomplete. *Logos* is revalued as a tool in the service of the limitless expression of the supreme power of human animality that sets man as a god over the other beasts competing for the earth's scarce goods. The world Nietzsche would release man for is one that paradoxically defies interpretation and valuation. It is fully real only at the moment that it dawns wholly formed and immanent within the vision of man. What is over man is no longer the world but a void as fathomless as though the world itself had not been called into Being.

IV. TIME, BEING, AND MORTALITY: TOWARDS THE OVERCOMING OF 'RESSENTIMENT'

A. Introduction

In Chapter One, we examined the lived experience of 'ressentiment' in its everydayness as found within Dostoevsky's 'Notes from the Underground'. Our investigation of the lived experience of 'ressentiment' demonstrated the necessity for proving the hermeneutical matrix within which this phenomenon has emerged. This led us to a careful consideration of the hermeneutics of 'ressentiment' in the philosophy of Max Scheler. In addition to sharpening the focus of the language used to talk about the phenomenon of 'ressentiment', our investigation of Scheler helped to resurface the social matrix within which the phenomenon makes its appearance in everyday life. We examined Scheler's own solution to the problem and found it wanting, especially because it could not account for the ontological conditions governing the possible appearance of the phenomenon.

In Chapter Three, we examined the underlying metaphysical foundations of Nietzsche's theory of 'ressentiment'. We examined Nietzsche's assertion that the ultimate ground of 'ressentiment' was man's relation to his own finitude and temporality. We considered, and found wanting, Nietzsche's own proposed solution to the problem.

In Chapter Four, we shall argue that Heidegger's phenomenological ontology promises to secure Nietzsche's fundamental insight concerning the rancor against time by offering a reconceived theory of the nature of time and being that suggests a theory of time and being without its wellsprings in 'ressentiment'. We shall emphasize selected portions of Heidegger's last work, "Time and Being", as presenting his most mature reflection on the subject.

B. The Temporality of Being

Unlike Dostoevsky, or Scheler or Nietzsche, Heidegger is concerned, even obsessed, to place his philosophic reflections within the matrix of what he conceives to be the authentic, dynamic unfolding of the history of philosophy. As is the case with Dostoevsky, his point of departure is always the immediate existential situation from out of which reflective thought emerges, and to which it must return for its ultimate validation. With Nietzsche, Heidegger is concerned to rediscover the dynamic set of meanings which constitute the world of reflection, with special emphasis on the time of philosophy's first beginnings. Unlike Dostoevsky, Heidegger is at pains always to purify through reflection the most pervasive patterns and structures within which the knots and contradictions of the life of everydayness appear. Unlike Nietzsche, Heidegger is concerned with submitting phenomenological intuition and metaphysical speculation to the most rigorous kind of critical demands. With Scheler, Heidegger shares a contempt for the ruling customs, beliefs, and institutions of modern Western life. Unlike Scheler, Heidegger is always concerned with problems of method and self-referentiality in which the questioner is called upon to answer for those questions which he asks, his way to finding the answer, as well as the answers themselves.

The task which Nietzsche bequeathes to philosophy is to found an ontology that will do justice to his insight concerning the rancor against time. The task which Heidegger sets himself in 'Being and Time' is no less than the phenomenological description of what it means to be human (*Dasein*).

The two-fold thrust of Nietzsche's investigation into the phenomenon of 'ressentiment' has revealed that it is time itself which serves to ground the unity of all possible appearances of rancor and the companion 'ressentiment'-laden interpretation of Being. The investigation of what it means to be human focuses on the inseparable relation of Being and time. Provisionally, we have described, following Nietzsche, the 'ressentiment' against Being as issuing from, as in the sense of caused by, the rancor against time. However, Nietzsche's analysis leaves open the question of what Being itself means. As such, the relation between Being and beings remains veiled. While we know that the will-to-power is expressive of the meaning of beings and that the doctrine of eternal return is advanced to thematize the existence of beings, the relation between Being and meaning remains to be clarified.

In the preface to 'Being and Time', Heidegger raises, with stunning simplicity, the question of the meaning of Being: "Do we in our time have an answer to the question of what we really mean by the word 'being'? Not at all. So it is fitting that we should raise anew *the ques-*

tion of the meaning of Being"[262]. Heidegger asserts that this question has ontological primacy over all others. It is implicit in every question asked, in every answer given, in every project undertaken, in every interpretation offered. Stated most simply, Heidegger's thesis may be expressed if we reflect upon the existential unity of what it means to be as I *am*.

The interrogatives "who" and "what" imperceptibly run together in ordinary discourse when one is asked to describe oneself. More often than not, the answer expected is framed in terms of what I am, with the pronominal "I" thought to be capable of being captured within a network of predicates that somehow divest the subject of his identity, much in the same way that garments could be disburdened one after the other. The very fact that a pause ensues upon the demand for giving a description of that self which I *am* suggests an existential distance between the fact that I *am* and the thematization of that same fact.

According to Heidegger, the nature of the "I am" or *sum*[263] has been systematically submerged in the history of philosophy, and, for this reason, the nature of knowledge about the self has remained abstract and superficial. The discrepancy between all accounts of the self I am, even those which I offer, and the existential reality of being myself results from the inability to reckon successfully with the question of what it means *to be* in the manner in which I am. The question seems, and is in fact, according to Heidegger, a circular one. This in no way invalidates the question, but, rather, on the contrary, helps to expose its essence. The dim awareness of what it is to be the being who I am ontologically precedes any thematic analysis of that same subject. It is to that tentative, vague region of existential immediacy that I must ever return for verification of all conceptual elaborations.

Heidegger defines man as the "being" who cares about his own being because he cares about Being[264]. It is the work of 'Being and Time', in part, to explore the patterns and structures of what it means to be as man is. The existential character of being human is itself described, according to Heidegger, within the horizon of a preconceptual understanding of the ontological conditions which give rise to the unified appearance of man's being.

Heidegger's analysis deepens the phenomenological reflection set in motion by Husserl. The intentional character of judgment and cognition is examined within the context of the life-world of everyday experience within which man's cognitive life emerges, manifests itself, and endures. To expose, as Nietzsche has, the fact that it is constitutive of man's being to be possessed by his corporeality, his passions, and his existence — as well as his intellect — requires a kind of explanation that Nietzsche's own analysis is not prepared to give.

Every axiom in Nietzsche's anti-metaphysical system is reintroduced by Heidegger in 'Being and Time' as an existential question in search of resolution. Consider the following: 1) Man suffers from time; 2) rancor against time results from what is perceived to be an unwarranted suffering caused by time; 3) the 'ressentiment'-laden valuations of being result from 2); 4) the 'ressentiment'-laden valuation against becoming results from the recognition that the essential structure of 3) is nothingness. The inner essence of what it means to be human is revealed as nihilism when the dynamic inter-relation of 1) through 4) is made manifest.

It is evident, especially from his later writings, that Heidegger does not dispute the existential character of Nietzsche's description of how man has experienced himself as appropriated by 'Sein' in the West and how the thematization of 'Sein' has been so reckoned as to disclose nothingness as the existential essence of 'Dasein'. What Heidegger asks is this: What kind of structure has been deformed, in the relatedness of Being to man, such that it is meaningfully possible to speak of 'ressentiment'-laden valuation of Being at all? Who is it that can speak about himself in such a way? What is Being such that its meaning can be so devalued? What is the temporal structure of existence such that authentic becoming can be transfigured by the rancor against time?

The essential thrust of Heidegger's investigation is to demonstrate that the description of human existence has been falsified by likening man to an object of reflection on the model of the natural sciences and to describing his existence as though one were categorizing aspects of an entity belonging to the natural world[265]. The objectification of man by man has concealed a more intimate knowledge which man has of his own situation. Heidegger's project is to describe with meticulous care the patterns and structures of everyday existence and to ask what the nature of being is such that this everydayness can make itself manifest[266]. If 'ressentiment' represents a deformed way of reckoning the meaning of beings encountered in everyday existence, what authentic structure does it in fact deform? This implies that there must exist an authentic temporality that the rancor against time misunderstands and deforms. The 'ressentiment' against becoming makes sense if and only if Being can itself be shown to become. At stake in these questions is an implicit reckoning with the question of the meaning of Being.

The various forms and guises of inauthentic being stem, on Heidegger's account, from an unwillingness to see that they are all flights from the perceived nothingness of Being.

"The utter insignificance which makes itself known in the 'nothing and nowhere', does not signify that the world is absent, but tells us that entities within-the-world are of so little importance in themselves that on the basis of this *significance* of what is within-the-world, the world in its worldhood is all that still obtrudes itself."[267]

Why should the question of 'ressentiment' against Being be relevant and meaningful for man unless he cares about the meaning of Being? Otherwise, the meaninglessness of beings would concern him not at all.

For Heidegger, Nietzsche's thinking represents the culmination of occidental metaphysics rather than a new beginning. It breaks ground in philosophy only for one who recognizes that Nietzsche's thought moves within the compass of traditional ontological assumptions concerning the nature of man, world, and Being[268]. Heidegger's existential analytic aims, in part, at demonstrating that the entire history of philosophy from Plato to Nietzsche rests upon the confusion of the existence of man with that of natural objects. It is this same philosophic confusion which, according to Heidegger, has dominated reflection on the nature of time.

The basic distinction which Heidegger makes in 'Being and Time' is between the mathematical and the existential concepts of time which he renders as "the static" and the "ecstatic" respectively. The static concept of time treats all time as 1) homogeneous, 2) continuous, and, at least from a theoretical standpoint, consisting of 3) units that are infinitely divisible. The conventional measurements of time taken by watches, calendars, etc. measure a time that is indifferent to and in that sense extrinsic of human concerns. Static time can be mapped with a series of points on a perpendicular Cartesian coordinate system. Time is homogenous, on this account, because there is no genuine qualitative difference demarcating the experienced phases of time. Here, concepts such as past, present, and future are mere psychological projections upon a substratum which is itself neutral to any such distinctions[269].

Secondly, static time is uninterrupted. Just as the seconds on a

clock tick off inexorably, just as the years on a calendar flow by
succeeding one another as marchers in a parade without end, static
time puts the lie to any attempt to distinguish authentic periods of
duration. Finally, when Heidegger says that static time is infinitely
divisible he means that it can most precisely be characterized as a
series of "nows" that correspond to points in a line that can always
be further subdivided.

It is important to point out here that Heidegger assigns an irreducible ontological status to the static concept of time, even though
his characterization is inexplicit[270]. The static concept of time, while
not reducible to natural or biological rhythms, does mirror in a manner more or less adequate to the most scientific discoveries, an accurate reflection of the inter-locking cosmological clocks of the
natural world.

Heidegger's contribution to the theory of time comes in his
description of ecstatic temporality[271]. Ecstatic temporality is 1)
heterogeneous, 2) discontinous, and 3) characterizable in terms of
phases that are non-reducible. Ecstatic temporality is measured in
terms of human care. It corresponds to what Bergson and James
called experienced time. Yet, there are differences both in Heidegger's
description of "experienced time" and the ontological status which
he accords it. Heidegger refuses Bergson's radical Heraclitean description of experienced time as an onrushing current, the tide of which is
one-directional and the orientation of which is irreducible[272]. Secondly, as has been remarked, he accords an ontological status to the concept of static temporality. The vital issue here concerns Heidegger's
assertion that ecstatic temporality exercises an ontological priority
over that kind of time that can be mapped out with Cartesian co-
ordinates. The most important practical implication of Heidegger's
positioning of the two kinds of time is his assertion that experienced
time cannot be dismissed as a psychological projection that is subjective, groundless, lacking in certitude, and arbitrary.

Both static time and ecstatic temporality are perceived by 'Dasein' as possible ways of being. That 'Dasein' experiences the hours of
his days and the days of the years of his life as distinguishable in a
qualitative manner, as oriented and dis-oriented, as longer and shorter,
is a report not simply about the experiences that occur "within" time,
but rather about the way in which he stands related to time itself.

In his later work post-dating the publication of 'Being and Time',
'Kant and the Problem of Metaphysics', Heidegger inserts his reflec-

tion on temporality into the history of philosophy. Heidegger argues that Kant, through the agency of the productive imagination which appears only in the "A" addition of the 'Critique of Pure Reason', has already grasped the phenomenon of ecstatic temporality, only to recoil from the power of his own insight in the "B" edition.[273]

The 'Critique of Pure Reason' takes up the task of demonstrating the capacity of the understanding to synthesize the sensuous data received from the realm of intuition. The transcendental aesthetic describes any given act of receptivity of sensuous data by the understanding by showing that space and time must be arranged in such a manner as to make it possible for the understanding to synthesize the impressions which it derives from intuition. In order to precisely determine the role of the productive imagination in relation to time, it is necessary to rethink Kant's discussion of the transcendental aesthetic. Time is distinguished from space as the inner sensibility which grounds the very appearance of the understanding. It is empirically real and transcendentally ideal[274].

For Kant, according to Heidegger, this means that the constituting power of time is decisive in determining the manner in which space, and all of the beings which appear in space, are synthesized and ordered for the understanding. Experience is real only in so far as it is possible. It is possible only insofar as it can be understood, i.e., rendered meaningful. The transcendental ideality of time signifies that the transcendental unity of apperception is capable of constituting synthetic units of meaning, the data of which are derived from sensuous impressions, and the concepts of which are formed from the understanding acting upon the pre-organized sensous data — only insofar as the activity of synthesizing on its manifold levels appears in a temporal manner[274].

The key question for Kant, as Heidegger interprets it, then, is: what determines the specificity of the selective interest in regard to the domain of sensous intuition? This is the same question which a Humean could respond with in the face of Kant's critique of Hume's epistemology. More precisely, why does the transcendental unity of apperception synthesize selected units of meaning rather than others? From the vantage point of the second edition of the 'Critique of Pure Reason' this remains a question within the psychological domain. It is concerned with judgments that are synthetic *a posteriori*. However, the first edition offers an explanation that is within the compass of critical or philosophic reflection. While each edition ascribes the function of apprehension and recognition to the transcendental imagination, only the "A" edition speaks of the existence and implied function of the productive imagination[275].

Heidegger asserts that Kant is maintaining that the productive imagination renders the synthesis of the understanding temporal. The introduction of the productive imagination makes it possible to account for the appearance of impressions given by the sensuous data of intuition shaped by the categories of the transcendental deduction insofar as these impressions are ordered as 'events' apprehended by the understanding. To borrow the language of Husserl, the noematic correlative of the productive imagination is time itself[276].

The work of the productive imagination, then, consists in the ever-recurring synthesis of the two modes of the transcendental aesthetic, assigning the priority of time over space. The essential features of space — positionality, proximity, extensionality are comprehended within the horizon of temporality — succession, simultaneity, etc.

The productive imagination is the very stance or orientation of the understanding itself as expressed in relation to the transcendental aesthetic. In this manner understanding betrays itself as perspectival by manifesting an orientation towards the perceptual world which it perpetually inherits from the sensuous data of intuition, modified by the judgments derived from the work of the categories of the transcendental deduction.

The non-relativity of the understanding at the level of judgment is grounded by an ulterior awareness derived from the perspectival, oriented understanding of given judgments in relation to the horizon of time. The productive imagination alone renders judgments comprehensible within the framework of events. In this sense, it actively achieves the schematism of the transcendental imagination by prefiguring the emergence of appearances within the unfolding horizon of human time[277].

The origination of any possible configuration of events from out of the chaotic, buzzing, blooming confusion of the sensory manifold cannot be explained without the foundational work of the productive imagination. If the role which Kant appears to assign to the productive imagination is taken seriously then the 'Critique of Pure Reason' shows — at least in the "A" edition — reason not only delimited and hence possible, but oriented and in that sense, actual.

In 'Being and Time' Heidegger takes up the theme which Kant

elaborates in the "A" deduction and develops a theory of Being which unfolds as time. In 'Introduction to Metaphysics', Heidegger situates this problem within the history of metaphysics; Heidegger explicitly sees himself elaborating the theory of time that, according to Heidegger, Kant advances in the first edition of the 'Critique of Pure Reason'. In order to ascribe ontological status to the ecstatic mode of temporality, Heidegger must be able to account for the reality of time past, time not yet, and a present that is somehow extended. From the vantage point of static temporality time past and time yet to be are non-existent. Nietzsche has brilliantly exploited the insight which Kant has both advanced and recoiled from in the "A" and "B" editions of the 'Critique of Pure Reason'. At the same time, Nietzsche adopted, in an uncritical manner, the position that holds static temporality to be ontologically primary.

The problem must be addressed on several levels. To begin with, how does 'Dasein' experience the past which is no longer and the future which is not yet? Heidegger asserts that 'Dasein' recognizes a past and a future that influence and inform the present.

It is incumbent upon Heidegger to demonstrate how an ecstatic temporality is possible for 'Dasein', if he is to maintain that the past and future can be secured against the interpretation of their virtual non-existence. The veracity of Heidegger's assertion depends upon the eliciting of those conditions necessary and sufficient to account for the existence of the past and the future of 'Dasein'. All alternatives that make covert or explicit reference to the power of memory or of anticipation will explain nothing on an ontological level simply because that which is remembered or anticipated cannot be understood as making what, for Heidegger, is the impossible transition from nothing to being. For this reason he cannot say that ecstatic temporality derives from the capacity of 'Dasein' to work upon or alter time comprehended in the static mode which, in advance of any such modification, assigns the past and the future to non-being.

The static concept of temporality makes an implicit interpretation that, insofar as the phases of time can be accredited with any ontological status, their unfolding is in a single direction from past to present to future. However, the events that happen upon 'Dasein' in his everydayness defy the linear unfolding of time from past to present to future. 'Dasein' always finds himself oriented towards the world in such a way as to find the world in front of him. The world presents itself in the guise of a question that asks 'Dasein' how he will cope with that which is immediately ahead of him. According to Heidegger it is 'Dasein' himself who is always ahead of himself, not into, but as the future of his own being. 'Dasein' speaks without knowing in advance precisely what he will say. However many rehearsals he may engage in, there comes a recognition of an uncontrolled spontaneity which admits of no advance script and from out of which 'Dasein' speaks.

According to the static concept of temporality, speech must be explained as moving from past to present to future. Here, 'Dasein' experiences speech as something he has which derives from an earlier thought which the grammar of speech clothes and the expression of language intends. At each moment a thought is born which becomes past the moment speech adequate to thought emerges in the present. Then, as an after thought one determines what to do with, or to whom to address, one's thoughts. The aim or intention of speech is, on this account, posterior to its emergence and external to the origination of thought. In an actual situation in which there is a speaker and a listener both would be understood in the act of perpetually rewinding the inner clock of speech awaiting their turn to engage in soliloquies which may somehow, and then quite by accident, penetrate the world of the other[278].

For Heidegger, inauthentic speech, which manifests itself as "idle talk" (*Gerede*), exhibits the time of inauthentic temporality[279]. It repeats formulas handed to it from the storehouse of language used by 'Das Man' whether or not such words are responsive to a given situation. The vital sense or direction of such language is, remarkably, the last consideration of such speech utterances[280].

The intention to convey or discover meaning in living speech discloses itself as requiring time for its emergence, appearance, and completion. The temporality of speech for the living moves from future to past through the present. The orientation towards that which remains to be said is the aperture through which the world of the speaker opens. Speech becomes incoherent just as it becomes disoriented, unaware of or unable to control where it is going. That which is unsaid, and in the view of static temporality, does not yet exist, discloses itself to the awareness of the living speaker as an absence that exerts a claim to become manifest. The absence which is the future of the utterance, now incomplete, is comprehended within the horizon of the promise of meaning which is to be achieved and actively binds together the phases of living speech. The meanings of the past, too, occur to the speaker as an absence that remains perpetually to be reanimated and integrated into the horizon of the speaker's ongoing conversation with himself in the face of the other, whether the other is personal or general, present or absent.

The units out of which the grammar of living speech emerge are discovered by the speaker ever again as posterior to the orientation and intention to achieve meaning. The alphabet can and does emerge in certain circumstances as a consideration of authentic speech, when for example, I wish to say something, and a word appears whose specific meaning I am unsure of, and for that reason discover myself as spelling the word to myself or to the other. In such a case the stringing together of the letters of the word emerges in order that we can be sure that we are hearing the same word.

Phenomenologically, we do not form complex units of meaning out of simpler particles. We do not move from privately held thoughts to words to the expression of words in combination. Much less do we go from letters of the alphabet to words and then sentences and combinations of sentences. We do not arrive at the present moment in which the word is spoken from out of a past that is prefigured and prepared for, and then find ourselves at the mercy of a future that just happens at the very next moment totally dumbfounded at its appearance. The static, chronological model of human temporality which moves in strict fashion from past to present to future through a series of successive now-points simply cannot do justice to the actuality of human speech.

Lost in the world of its immediate concerns, 'Dasein' substitutes idle talk for authentic speech, curiosity for authentic understanding, and ambiguity for resoluteness. *Dasein lives as though it were eternal.* For, in the language of 'Das Man', "Death certainly comes, but not right away"[281].

'Das Man', or fallen 'Dasein', does not deny the factuality of death; far from it, he establishes an island fortress in the midst of the knowledge of the inevitability of its withering assault. He prepares for its advent as does everyone by taking out "life insurance", purchasing a plot, and making suitable provisions so that he shall not make a nuisance of himself. Heidegger asserts that death comprehended from a standpoint of inauthenticity hides behind the fiction that because death comes for everyone, it is inherently a natural phenomenen[282]. Just as static time may be viewed after the aspects of a thing present-on-hand, so, too, may death be likened to an object or event in the natural world. The primary metaphors for speaking of death compare it to: 1) a stopping place at the end of a long road; 2) fruit that matures and ripens upon a tree; 3) paying off a last debt that is owed. The fact that death signals, by definition, the end of life permits the plausibility of such metaphors just because the concept of "end" is itself inherently ambiguous and open to multiple interpretations. For Heidegger the inauthentic stance towards death deprives 'Dasein' of the possibility of comprehending a two-fold recognition: a) the meaning of death as *my own* b) the knowledge of that nothingness which serves as the gateway through which Being is distinguished from beings. It is in concealing the constitutive structure of his finitude that 'Dasein', in the mode of 'Das Man' lives, against his professed understanding, as though he were eternal.

Heidegger advances an epistemological argument in order to being his point home. Husserl's concept of intentionality has been rendered ontological in 'Being and Time'. Heidegger describes the field of 'Dasein's' existence as self-transcending, meaning that every act of understanding reveals an object of intentional awareness. 'Dasein' discovers himself as situated in the world and his awareness as opening on to the beings of the world. Only when he grasps the nothingness of death is 'Dasein' without an intentional object, thereby opening him to the recognition that his awareness of nothingness serves as a ground against which the figures of all the beings of the world emerge[283].

Freed of its peculiar Heideggerian speech, the epistemological argument may be transposed into a more conventional philosophical idiom. If I am able to describe the knowledge which I have of any entity X, then one condition for my being able to give a report of such knowledge is my being able to give a description in terms of those predicates ascribable to the subject X. For example, if I wish to report my knowledge of a fugitive, I may say that he is tall or short, thin or fat, male or female. My knowledge about him is inexact just to the extent that I am unable to fill in the details of such a description. Were I to say, on the other hand, that I had 'knowledge' about him but was unable to predicate a single adjective of the subject, then surely I would be using the word 'knowledge' in an overly enthusiastic and less than exact manner.

If the knowledge that I have of my own death is truly of a kind of nothingness, then it would seem true by definition to say that I can make no significant knowledge claims about it. Moreover, as Epicurus stressed long ago, any presumed knowledge that I could be said to

have of my own death presupposes the existence of my living awareness as a covert, and hence impossible, spectator.

It is through the mood of anxiety that 'Dasein' grasps the nothingness of his finitude. Anxiety is possessed of cognitive significance for
Heidegger, meaning that, at the same time, it provides no specific in-
formation about any being in the world. Anxiety informs 'Dasein'
concerning the ground of his world against which the meanings of
beings emerge. Heidegger insists that moods are improperly understood when we think of them as signifying merely the atmosphere of
psychological environment within which objective conceptual understanding emerges. On Heidegger's view, there is no single act of understanding that is not accompanied by a mood. The manner in which
mood "accompanies" understanding reveals mood as constitutive of
understanding.

Heidegger refuses to say that moods merely color our acts of
understanding and in that sense remove us from an objective comprehension of states of affairs. The function of any mood, for Heidegger,
is to tune us in to the ground of the world in whose midst we find
ourselves situated[284]. In the case of anxiety, Heidegger draws on a distinction between fear and anxiety that is now commonplace in psychology[285]. Fear finds itself always possessed by an object in the presence of which 'Dasein' recognizes himself as fearful. Anxiety, on the
other hand, is defined by the absence of any given object.

Anxiety is the singular state of mind in which the possibility of
permanent non-being presents itself to 'Dasein'. The mood of anxiety
uproots 'Dasein' from his world. In anxiety the being-there, 'Dasein',
no longer has a sure and immediate grasp on what it means to be
there. In the mode of his everydayness 'Dasein' experiences his being-
there as caught up in, and in that sense lost within, the multiple concerns that are exhaustive of the particular meanings of his world.

Anxiety, in revealing the prospect of permanent nothingness,
simultaneously discloses to 'Dasein' his radical finitude and the dreadful recognition that the meaning of Being is not *given*. The ontological
difference between Being and beings remains concealed in the exces-
sive solicitude which 'Dasein' has for the beings in its immediate environment. The awareness of his own finitude is something that remains removed from the present and always beyond the horizon of his
understanding of, and concern for, beings. For Heidegger, the recognition that there is a difference between Being and beings, the *ontological difference*, is accompanied by this dreadful recognition that the

meaning of Being is not given. This occasions an awareness on the part of 'Dasein' of the radical indeterminacy of the meaning of his fate. In this respect, anxiety alone opens to 'Dasein' the possibility of philosophy. Philosophy is inseparable from the power given to 'Dasein' to interpret and determine the course of what in retrospect is called his fate.

The recognition of his mortality becomes an ontological problem of the whole and its parts only when 'Dasein' understands that Being challenges him with the demand of becoming whole. The meaning of Being determines how 'Dasein' comports himself with beings. His anxiety results directly from the recognition that the ontological difference affords him the challenge and burdens him with the task of determining the meaning of Being, and standing steadfast against the knowledge of nothingness that overlays his relation with all beings.

Standing steadfast in the face of the knowledge of finitude, Heidegger characterizes as "anticipatory resoluteness"[286]. It is by displaying such resoluteness that 'Dasein' achieves existential unity over the unfolding of ecstatic temporality. The existential solution to the rancor against time is re-solved in the "moment of vision" when 'Dasein' grasps the project of his becoming unified and whole.

Just as the doctrine of eternal return of same gives way to the phenomenon of ecstatic temporality, so too, does Nietzsche's "supraman" yield to authentic, i.e., resolute 'Dasein'. Is the rancor against time and the 'ressentiment' against Being overcome with such a solution?

Heidegger impales himself on the protruding horns of the dilemma created by his own radical questioning: "But on what basis does Dasein disclose in resolution? On what is it to resolve? Only the resolution can give the answer."[287] The knowledge of permanent nothingness creates a stance of resoluteness. Yet, it does nothing to inform the understanding of the steps to be taken on the way to becoming.

Anticipatory resoluteness, its possibility grounded in ecstatic temporality, moves towards the overcoming of the rancor against time. It permits us to see how man can promise, how word can become truly constitutive of deed. For the future can be taken into the present, and thereby made constitutive of it. The past, too, is preserved in the meanings of the possibilities that still dwell ahead of 'Dasein', and are thereby open to the bending of his resolve.

An adequate existential solution to the rancor against time depends upon an ontological resolution to the 'ressentiment' against Being.

Here, the thought of 'Being and Time' still moves within the circle of 'ressentiment'. 'Dasein', however resolved, has yet to grasp how the knowledge of nothingness can serve to ground the meaningful appearance of beings. Why should 'Dasein' wish to be resolved, if the meaning of any given being is to be determined solely on the basis of his will-to-power? The phenomenon of nothingness still waits upon revaluation. The Being of time must be rethought. Otherwise, the phenomenon of ecstatic temporality, the mood of anxiety, and anticipatory resoluteness in the face of finitude will remain within the circle of 'ressentiment', because nothingness is still indistinguishable from Being.

C. The Being of Time

Not until the very late essay "On Time and Being" does Heidegger offer his most explicit statement on how it is that time is to be reconceived when the phenomenon of Being has been rethought to its roots. The rancor against time derives from the recognition of time's passing. The 'ressentiment' against Being issues from the devaluation of that which passes because it is fated to the temporal:
"What is in time and is thus determined by time, we call the temporal. When a man dies and is removed from what is here, from beings here and there, we say that his time has come. Time and the temporal mean what is perishable, what passes away in the course of time. . . . For time itself passes away."[288]
Heidegger distinguishes time from the temporal. All that is in time, and thus determined by time, he characterizes as "the temporal". What is always essential to time is that it passes away and that it passes away constantly. It is the constancy of the passing away of time that forces a reconsideration of the Being of time. Because, "by passing away constantly, time remains as time"[289]. What, Heidegger asks, does it mean for time to be possessed of constancy, to remain? For to ask this question is to inquire after the very Being of time.
The answer can be rendered in a formula: "To remain means: not to disappear, thus, to presence"[290]. However, Heidegger admonishes that we distance ourselves from a true comprehension of the meaning of presence and the present if we assume that the presence of the present is to be identified with the passing "now"[291]. In fact, the passing

"now" can itself, Heidegger implies, only be determined in terms of the concept of presence:

"If such were the case, the present as presence and everything which belongs to such a presence would have to be called real time, even though there is nothing immediately about it of time as time is usually represented in the sense of a succession of a calculable sequence of nows."[292]

Negatively, this means that the concept of presence is understood only in an ontologically derivative manner when determined in terms of duration, measured in terms of its capacity to "last" from one "now" to the next. Yet, to remain, to be constant, means to last, to hold out, to endure. How is it that the presence of the present can be said to endure, when time in its wholeness has been defined as that which passes away?

Unlike the "now" that belongs to the present conceived as something on hand, presence is defined by Heidegger as "the constant abiding that approaches man, reaches him, is extended to him"[293]. Presence, then, belongs to the future and the past as well as the present. As Heidegger says about the past: "What has been does not just vanish from the previous now as does that which is merely past. Rather, what has been presences, but in its own way. In what has been, presencing is extended."[294] Also, with regard to the future, Heidegger refuses the provisional characterization of it as that which is not-yet: "In the future, in what comes toward us, presencing is offered."[295]

By the time of the appearance of the essay under consideration, Heidegger appears to have abandoned all pretense of methodological justification. He explicity affirms that his procedure is not to be confused with the method of dialectic, which he insists presupposes the traditional concepts of Being and time, which he sets himself the task of rethinking. He refuses, moveover, to classify the inquiry into the Being of time as phenomenological in character, although he presupposes familiarity on the part of the reader with the phenomenological ontology set out in 'Being and Time'. Although the now famous 'Kehre', or turn, in Heidegger's approach to philosophy from phenomenology to 'Denken', or thinking, does not mean that previously stringent criteriological considerations, once binding, are now absent, Heidegger makes statements in "On Time and Being" that, considered out of context, support this simplistic interpretation that would equate the activity of 'Denken' with groundless and apparently arbitrary intuition:

"But how can we become properly involved with this matter at stake named by the titles 'Being and time', 'time and Being'?

Answer: by cautiously thinking over the matters named here. Cautiously means at first: not hastily invading the matters with unexamined notions, but rather reflecting on them carefully.

But may we take Being, may we take time, as matters? They are not matters, if 'matter' means: something which is. The word 'matter', 'a matter', should mean for us now what is decisively at stake in that something inevitable is concealed within it. Being — a matter, presumably *the* matter of thinking.

Time — a matter, presumably *the* matter of thinking, if indeed something like time speaks in Being as presence. Being *and* time, time *and* Being, name the relation of both issues, the matter at stake which holds both issues toward each other and endures their relation. To reflect upon this situation is the task of thinking, assuming that thinking remains intent on persisting in its matter."[296]

The activity of 'Denken' can proceed just because 'Sein' is what thinking always opens upon, and that which it is determining in any of its given manifestations. The implicit argument that Heidegger makes concerning the inseparability of thinking and Being represents a continuation and deepening of Kant's transcendental method of grounding the possibility of factual appearances.

From a standpoint that is concerned with evaluating the logical coherence, consistency, and validity of competing and contradictory deductive syllogisms, it would be necessary to point out that Nietzsche and Heidegger begin with differing major premises concerning the Being of time, and, therefore, come to equally valid, if totally opposed, conclusions. When Heidegger asserts that the past and the future as well as the present are possessed of Being, understood as presence, this seems a no more warrantable assertion than the one supposed by Nietzsche, that past and future are *not*. If we are prepared to concede Heidegger's starting point, then it would seem that the two-fold problem of the rancor against time and the 'ressentiment' against Being can be easily resolved by making adjustments in the realm of speech. If the past and the future are possessed of Being, then the nothingness which, for Nietzsche, grounds the rancor against time's passing, will be overcome. In place of that which is no more, there is now the abiding of time in its very passing away. The 'ressentiment' against

Being derives from the experience of the loss of meaning that is thought to belong together with the virtual non-existence of the past and the future. The abiding character of that which passes, even in its passing, can alone serve to ground the possibility of a revaluation of the meaning of Being.

To assert that Being abides in its passing requires demonstration. What kind of demonstration will produce a satisfactory resolution? If we stay within the limits of speech alone, substituting Being for nothingness, presence for non-existence, etc., then clearly a linguistic victory over 'ressentiment' can be won instantenously with the appearance of a handy formula. We may wish to say that Nietzsche has presented philosophy with a false problem that has arisen from an improper usage of language and a generalized misunderstanding of the capacity of words to reveal the truth about phenomena. But a merely linguistic solution to the problem leaves unanswered the kind of existential dilemma faced by Dostoevsky's man from underground. The problem posed by the rancor against time demands an existential resolution. The possibility of providing such a resolution depends, it its turn, on the capacity of Being to manifest itself in the manner indicated by Heidegger if the realm of speech is to reveal meanings that are also able to abide. This is what Nietzsche had in mind when he said that "nothing is easier to erase than a dialectical effect", and why Heidegger condemns the dialectical procedure in philosophy as premature[297].

The overcoming of the 'ressentiment' against Being cannot be won in a instant. It requires time. This, in turn, supposes that Being, in its abiding, gives itself as time that unfolds. The primordial injury which man experiences at the hands of the passing of time must itself be capable of being redressed. It is not necessary or even possible to overcome 'ressentiment' against the factual character of the temporal, as Nietzsche professes, by promising the illusion of an unreal and inauthentic self-transcendence. It is Being itself that must ground the possibility of the overcoming of 'ressentiment' as well as occasioning the way designated by its appearance. No less is required than that thinking repose in Being in order that the dialectical opposition between Being and thinking may emerge. How is it that the simultaneous demand for the coincidence and contraposition of Being and thinking can be satisfied? Is there a single unitary ground in which the two-fold movement of self-coincidence and self-opposition can manifest itself as the Being of time?

Heidegger discovers the underlying unity of Being and time as that which makes the ontologically irreducible unit of an "event" itself possible. The question which we could not refrain from asking of Nietzsche, how out of the ceaseless stream of becoming are configurable events possible, Heidegger resolves to answer:
"What determines both, time and Being in their own, that is, in their belonging together, we shall call: *Ereignis*, the event of Appropriation. *Ereignis* will be translated as Appropriation or event of Appropriation. One should bear in mind, however, that 'event' is not simply an occurrence but that which makes any occurrence possible. What this word names can be thought now only in the light of what becomes manifest in our looking ahead toward Being and toward time as destiny and as extending, to which time and Being belong."[298]

What does Heidegger mean when he states that Being itself is to be understood as the event of Appropriation? Heidegger explicitly warns that "Appropriation is not the encompassing general concept under which Being and time could be subsumed"[299]. In asking after the nature of the event of Appropriation, Heidegger regards the question of whether Being is to be considered a species of Appropriation irrelevant in the sense that the demand for taxonomical classification is premature. The primary impulse in the asking of the question aims at awakening reflection on the matter of those conditions which govern the possible appearance of any given factual occurence, event, or being. Heidegger regards his own inquiry concerning the nature of Being as belonging to the metaphysical tradition of the West and as exposing that which has remained concealed, and yet controlling, within the history of the activity of metaphysics. What has remained concealed, as Heidegger teaches in every one of his books, is the pervasive tendency to think about beings and to leave the phenomenon of Being unthought.

What is "It", Heidegger asks, that governs the possible appearances and transformations that have bestowed an epochal character and identity on the meaning of Being? In the 'Introduction to Metaphysics' Heidegger first presented the history of Being as it had undergone decisive transformation from Plato's representation of Being as *idea* to Aristotle's representation of Being as *energeia*, to Kant's rendering of it as *position*, to Hegel's understanding of Being as *absolute concept*, and lastly to Nietzsche's doctrine of Being expressed as the *Will-to-Power*. In succeeding explorations, Heidegger has detailed each of these epochal transformations in the history of philosophy[300]. What remains the same from Plato to Nietzsche, Heidegger affirms, is the absorption of the phenomenon of presence into the concept of the present[301]. To be possessed of reality means, for the whole of the western tradition, according to Heidegger, to be actual, complete, self-identical, motionless, and therefore timeless, and hence "eternal". Only in Nietzsche's doctrine of the eternal recurrence of same is this governing ontological assumption rendered explicit. The truth of Being, as understood by the Plato of the later dialogues, is approached in direct relation to the capacity of concrete beings to image the unchanging and invariant forms of the *eide*, which in turn is thought by Plato to insure the configurations of the beings that are. The reality of each being may be determined at any given instant just insofar as it may be rightly said to participate in the Being of the deathless *eide*.

What is it that remains one and self-same such that there can be imperishable essences? What, for man, does it mean for anything to be? Heidegger believes that all authentic philosophy aims at resolving this question yet has failed of its resolution because the question is prematurely deflected onto the realm of particular beings. The horizon within which this most fundamental question of metaphysics is fated to reappear belongs to the being of time. It is the representation of the unity of time which Heidegger disputes in the case of Plato and in what he regards to be Aristotle's decisive characterization of time for the western philosophical tradition. Boldly, Heidegger asks a question that must seem the paradigm of a category mistake: "But where is time? *Is* time at all and does it have a place? Obviously, time is not nothing."[302] Transposed and reintegrated into the western tradition, Heidegger's question would read as follows: For Plato — where *are* the deathless *eide*? For Aristotle — where is *logos* wholly possessed by *nous*? Or where is *dynamis* wholly *energeia*? For Kant — where *is* the transcendental unity of apperception? For Hegel — where *is* the absolute concept? And, as we have asked after Nietzsche's doctrine of eternal return — where (and how) can it *be*? Common to the objections that can be entertained against these multiple "mistaken" questions is the implied belief that there is no place to look for the moment of the self-manifestation of reality because, being nowhere, it cannot be found.

The most apparent indication that a student of Plato or of Aristotle or of Kant or Hegel is misguided is evident when he confuses the categories of the temporal and the logical. Philosophic innocence has been left behind when the student of Hegel's 'Phenomenology of

Mind' leaves off demanding that he experience the Moment as though
it was possessed of duration, as though it were a Moment he might enjoy or pass or remember. The Moment is, for Hegel, a logical concept
or a dialectical one, or that which dialectic requires — a transcendental
one. It is not the stuff of which mere occurrences are possessed, or by
which they might be numbered. What does it mean for man to be appropriated by a trans-historical moment that empties him of that existence which betimes he calls his own?

Granted that the transcendental unity of apperception is the irreducible position, upon which the transcendental possibility of all
factual cognition depends for Kant, and recognizing that, to say the
ground of the unity of all cognition *is* — but not in the head or in the
world — what does it mean to say that it is in transcendental space or
more precisely, nowhere? What is this ultimate position that governs
all understanding and yet, is posited as the absence of positions? It is
this terrible complaint against the invisible that Nietzsche set out to
rectify, and in the process inverted the Socratic-Platonic-Aristotelian
world order. Banished to the realm of the invisible is the unity of *logos, taxis, dike*, and *to agathon* — thought, order, justice, and the
Good. In the quest for the essence of what it means to be human
(*anthropos*), now only the animal in man shines through and all that
is not appropriated by the sphere of vital values has become invisible.

According to Heidegger, it is the dual capacity of Being to reveal
and withhold itself that grounds the appearance of its concrete signification in any one of its epochal guises:
"Epoch does not mean here a span of time in occurrence, but rather
the fundamental characteristic of sending, the actual holding-back of
itself in favor of the discernibility of the gift, that is, of Being with
regard to the grounding of beings. The sequence of epochs in the
destiny of Being is not accidental. Still, what is appropriate shows itself in the belonging together of the epochs."[303]

Here Heidegger seeks to ground the historicity of being human
while avoiding the pitfall of naive historicism that would presuppose
the very answer that it sets out to resolve. It is not the phenomenon of
history that grounds the appearance of beings: but rather, the capacity
of Being to both give and withhold itself that establishes the possibility of the phenomenon of history.

When Heidegger asks "where is time?" he addresses the question
of the indissoluable unity of Being and time, the underlying unity of
the sending forth and the holding back of that which gives and that

which withholds the Being of time. The ancient paradox first articulated by Parmenides, the logical contradiction that prevails in the statement "One *is*", transposed by Plato into a reflection on the statement "Being *is* one" in the dialogue he named after Parmenides, is joined, by Heidegger, with a reflection on the nature of time. It is only on this terrain that the existential meaning of unity, that so confounds Dostoevsky's man from underground, and the metaphysical problem of unity, that shackles Nietzsche's overman in his attempt to escape the fetters imposed by the rancor against time, can be discovered. It is only by re-asking the problem of the One and the Many as it is found by man within time that Scheler's paradox of accounting for a multiplicity of others, and thus the possibility of addressing others as concrete, distinguishable beings, can be solved.

Both Nietzsche and Scheler assent to a theory of time in which past, present, and future are revealed at the same time, all at once. There is a submerged anger at that which withholds itself, in each thinker, that which will not manifest itself at the same time. Each commends a 'ressentiment' against past and future for a life lived wholly in the present. It is the fate of the man from underground that he cannot dwell fully in the present because of an obsessive preoccupation with the past and the future. Heidegger asks after the meaning of time and how it stands in the governing relation to man such that authentic self-contemporaneity is achievable? In recasting the question of the unity of time, he refuses an existentially disingenous denial of the presence of past and future: ". . . we must give the name 'time' to the unity of reaching out and giving . . . to this unity alone. For time itself is nothing temporal, no more than it is something that is. It is thus inadmissible to say that future, past and present are before us 'at the same time'."[304]

How is it, Heidegger asks, that time can be possessed of unity while offering the appearance of its three distinguishable dimensions? He states: "The unity of time's three dimensions consists in the interplay of each toward each. This interplay proves to be the true extending, playing in the very heart of time, the fourth dimension, so to speak – not only so to speak, but in the nature of the matter."[305] Heidegger reverses the metaphysical thrust of the Parmenidean paradox and Zeno's application of this same paradox in relation to time. Heidegger's point of departure remains, in this respect, unchanged from 'Being and Time'. Given the distinguishable and irreducible phases of time, how is it that each manages to endure while holding itself off from the rest? It is the ontological "givenness" of time to appear three dimensional that constitutes, for Heidegger, its fourth dimension:

"In future, in past, in the present that giving brings about to each its own presencing, holds them apart, thus opened and so holds them toward one another in the nearness by which the three dimensions remain near one another. For this reason we call the first, original, literally incipient extending in which the unity of true time consists 'nearing nearness', 'nearhood' (*Nahheit*), an early word still used by Kant. But it brings future, past and present near to one another by distancing them. For it keeps what has been open by denying its advent as present. This nearing of nearness keeps open the approach coming from the future by withholding the present in the approach. Nearing nearness has the character of denial and withholding. It unifies in advance the ways in which what has-been, what is about to be and the present reach out toward each other."[306]

The straining of speech about time results from the great difficulty in thinking through that which has been previously unthought. It is at the farthest remove from mere metaphorical foliage; rather, it seeks to recover the roots which permit us to render philosophically intelligible even the growth of the branches of scientific understanding. The commonly understood concept of the 'dimensionality of time', "thought as the succession of the sequence of nows, is borrowed from the representation of three-dimensional space"[307], and, therefore, requires that the appearance of dimensionality itself be accounted for and clarified.

Heidegger sets out to redefine the concept of "time-space" with the aim of demonstrating the possibility of unidimensionality as measured in terms of numbers and as represented by a line and parameter. He is not interested in disputing that this is the way in which "time-space" is commonly understood and the distance between two time-points is calculated. Rather, he is concerned with establishing how any area of possible measurement can make itself manifest such that it can be represented and delimited. This requires that the concept of presence, which may be represented as a point on a line, but which must be held to be a representation, first manifests the being of its presence. Even an indefinite series of present moments represented as points on a line do not, by themselves, reckon with the problem of the Being of any one of those states to which the now-points refer, or how they refer to those states capable of representation but not yet so represented.

Heidegger reconceives the phenomenon of time-space with the aim of showing how the phenomenological and mathematical aspects of the presence of the present belong together. Only in this way is it possible to demonstrate the very possibility of divergence of conceptual reflection from existential being. How can Being make room for space, unfold as space? This is another way in which Heidegger asks how presence can make itself manifest:

"Time-space now is the name for the openness which opens up in the mutual self-extending of futural approach, past and present. This openness exclusively and primarily provides the space in which space as we usually know it can unfold. The self-extending, the opening up, of future, past and present is itself prespatial. Only thus can it make room, that is, provide space."[308]

Without the capacity to unfold as future, past, and present, there could be no phenomenon of time as it is lived existentially. Dimensionality, the reciprocal relation by virtue of which the dimensions of time offer and withhold themselves from each other, governs the ontological unity grounding the possibility of the unified appearance of existential time. Only if the presence of time can be assured can the question which Heidegger asks, "Where is time?", be answered. It is one thing to affirm, as Heidegger does, the presence of future, past, and present and a different and more strenuous matter to demonstrate such an affirmation. Where is the presence of the future, the presence of the past? To affirm that the presence of the future belongs to the power of anticipation, that the presence of the past belongs to recollection, just as the presence of the present may be said to belong to perception, presupposes the answer in the act of explanation. What is *it* that anticipation, recollection, and perception gather up severally and together? Where are we to look for the being of the future and of the past? How does the presumed presence of the future and of the past make itself manifest?

D. The Phenomenology of Absence

Heidegger asks: "But what is the source of this extending reach to which the present belongs as presencing, insofar as there is presence? True, man always remains approached by the presencing of something actually present without explicitly heeding presencing itself. But we have to do with absence just as often, that is, constantly."[309] It is in the mode of absence that the future and the past appear. If we ask again where is the future, or where is the past, the answer which Heidegger gives is that they are *absent*. How can that which is said to be absent reveal itself as other than mere nothingness? It is the manner in which absence *is* that determines the dynamism and originality of Heidegger's reflection.

How is it that we can be said to have to do with the phenomenon of absence *constantly*? Here, Heidegger's spare and brilliant observations open the way to an uncharted enquiry, the surfacing of which can shed new light upon a previously unilluminated dimension of human existence. About the past which is no longer, Heidegger says: "And yet, even that which is no longer present presences immediately in its absence — in the manner of what has been, and still concerns us. What has been does not just vanish from the previous now as does that which is merely past. Rather, what has been presences, but in its own way. In what has been, presencing is extended."[310]

The absent past is distinguishable in the manner in which what has been dwells as a presence that approaches man constantly. There is a difference between that which has never been and is no longer, and that which once was and is now absent. If this most vital distinction cannot be ontologically sustained, then the difference between the living and dead, night and day, past and future, meaning and nonsense, and Being and nothingness cannot be made distinguishable.

At any given present moment, understood as a "now-point", the past is that which is understood as not-here-now. From the ripple of the immediate past moment breaking into ever broadening waves that have crested, broken, and disappeared we find the hour which can be counted but is no longer, the day that has vanished with twilight, the years leading up to the present one that are fled and gone, the epochs of historical time. Heidegger urges upon us the question of how it is that we distinguish a life that has been lived and is no longer from one that has never been. He asks us to inquire along with him as to how it can be that time lived and spent can be rendered distinguishable from a time that has never been. He asks us to ask how it is that the time of everyday existence, the time of history, the time of Being can and does endure.

The absent past appears in the present as a phenomenon that manifests itself through the peculiar appearance belonging to the nature of that which is absent. Quite obviously, Heidegger does not mean that absence signifies presence somewhere else. The absent past is not present except insofar as its absence manifests itself as an abiding presence. Heidegger describes this same capacity on the part of the future to reveal itself as an absence that approaches without abandoning itself in such a way as to make the past indistinguishable from the future:

"But absence also concerns us in the sense of what is not yet present in the manner of presencing in the sense of coming toward us. To talk of what is coming toward us has meanwhile become a cliche. Thus we hear: 'the future has already begun', which is not so, because the future never just begins since absence, as the presencing of what is not yet present, always in some way already concerns us, is present no less immediately than what has been. In the future, in what comes toward us, presencing is offered."[311]

What remains to be clarified is the precise manner in which absence manifests itself as a phenomenon in the multiple, distinguishable senses in which this word may be meaningfully employed while, at the same time, sustaining a sense of what remains the same about absence in its differing appearances. Here, Heidegger's intention to express the distinction between absence, understood as a positive mode of being, from the perjorative sense in which it is held to be a privative mode of being, is clearer than his own work in the service of validating such a distinction.

To speak, as Heidegger does, of absence, "as the presencing of what is not yet present", is already to register the difficulty of defining absence as other than a privative mode of being. It gives the impression that absence remains as an imperfect kind of presence, imperfect in respect to the presence that does belong to that which is now present. The standard for speech about absence is still reckoned in relation to the figure of the now-points that determines the present as something on hand. Clearly, this is not Heidegger's intention:

"If we heed still more carefully what has been said, we shall find in absence — be it what has been or what is to come — a manner of presencing and approaching which by no means coincides with presencing in the sense of the immediate present. Accordingly, we must note: Not every presencing is necessarily the present. A curious matter. But we find such presencing, the approaching that reaches us, in the present, too. In the present, too, presencing is given."[312]

The sense in which Heidegger uses the word absence (*Abwesenheit*) requires clarification, if the profound philosophic point he intends is to be appreciated. We say, in everyday English usage, that when an object is not in its expected place, and therefore, that it must be somewhere else — that it is absent. In searching for a book that is not in its accustomed place on the bookshelf, it is in compliance with the rules of English grammar to use the word "absent" as a predicate adjective synonymous with the word "missing". Or, if the presence of someone has been expected at a meeting, and the person is not in attendance, we say that the expected one is "absent". In both of these cases, applicable to objects as well as persons, the important point is that absence from one place implies presence in another.

The usage of the word "absence", while it admits of spatio-temporal identification, is not exhausted by this sense of the word. Take the example of the "new" moon. Every twenty-nine days the moon disappears from the view of the unaided human eye. Upon such occasions, as is the case when the moon is obscured by clouds, it is common to hear such expressions as "tonight there is no moon". This kind of statement is understood as one that is not meant literally. Here "literal" implies that the existence of a moon can be scientifically corroborated. To say that x is absent, and that x is the new moon indicates that while it is concealed from view from one observer (y) even all actual observers (as is the case during an eclipse), x nonetheless can be viewed by some (y) — i.e., actual observer — under conditions which permit visibility of x. To say about x that there is "no moon" in the sense that it is concealed from view, but known to exist, is a far different kind of assertion from the statement that is identical to it in form, "there is no moon", intending to affirm by this that the moon does not now, has not, or even will exist. Each statement is accompanied by a sense of nullity, but with emphatically different kinds of meaning. When Heidegger speaks of the concept of truth as *aletheia*, as the making manifest of that which has been concealed, it would seem that the truth is absent much in the same way that the new moon remains hidden from the unaided human eye[313]. That is to say, that the act of revealing the truth from its position of obscurity depends upon the capacity to sweep away the mists which envelop it in much the same manner that the clouds must roll away for the light of the moon to be made manifest.

However, the problem with speech about the absent past or the absent future raises a peculiar kind of problem that cannot be addressed by supposing that a privileged observer could somehow discover its presence, as though presence here were coincident with that which can be said to exist "now". It is not a matter of the absent past or future being somewhere else, as is the case with the missing book or person; nor is it the case that there are unfavorable conditions which interfere with visibility. And, unlike *aletheia* it is not a matter of plumbing depths which, in the nature of the case remain hidden from view, but always possessed of the presence of the present. For in all of these cases, the phenomenon of absence is unmasked as a privative mode of presence either displaced, obscured, or buried. What is absent can be made present in each of these cases by a change of position, perspective, or illumination.

The more radical sense of absence which Heidegger has in mind conditions the very possibility of presence and must be described in such a way as to be distinguishable from the presence that belongs only to the present. At the same time, it must satisfy the philosophic demand that makes it irreducible to a mere nullity. Here, Heidegger's suggestive statements on the phenomenon of absence demand elaboration.

To begin with, let us take the case of something which once was possessed of presence, but is no longer. Consider the case of romantic love which once seemed inextinguishable, and is, now, no longer. We rule out such cases as can be qualified by repositioning (as of the search for another love), or an alteration of perspective (romantic love, maturely understood must transform itself into something higher if it is to endure), or illumination (if only the two parties could understand each other more clearly). Let us assume that it is the love born of innocence which, as Socrates says in the 'Symposium', believes all beauty to repose in one other concrete being. To dwell here, in the absence of such love, means that the absence *as such* is recognizable and makes its way into the surrounding present through traces that cannot be filled in. There is no comfort that can be gained from the recognition that such a love can be found somewhere else, as for example, in the concept that links all romantic loves together. Either one laments an absence that is final and absolute or one forages for a new presence of love because the absence beheld is unbearable.

The case of a child who grieves over the loss of a parent offers an emphatic illustration of this same point. Surely, there is a dramatic difference between the death of a beloved father for a son and the meaning of that same death for someone, even another son, who knew the father not at all, although in both cases, from the standpoint of an

indifferent observer, the father is just as nonexistent. Neither repositioning, alteration of perspective, or the shedding of illumination can
alter lived experience in such a way as to compromise the distinction
between the keenly felt absence of the father who was loved by the
one son and the nonexistence of the father for the second son, who
knew him not.

To suppose the philosophic necessity of sustaining the distinction
between the phenomenon of absence and virtual nonexistence in order
to account for the possible appearance of beings is a different thing
from showing how absence, in fact, reveals itself. How do the primary
modes of absence become evident, make a claim upon our concernful,
waking lives?

The phenomenon of speech reveals silence as a primordial mode of
absence that is constitutive of the very possibility of living human
speech. Silence is something that we hear. It is not a mere nullity that
interrupts the otherwise incessant flow of speech and noise. The absence of speech is the horizon from out of which speech is sounded,
the background against which every audible echo resounds. Yet, to
one who hears not at all nor knows the confirmation of his own
speech, silence does not "sound" for it cannot be heard. Silence can
be heard because it lives in the expectation of speech.

Silence is possible only if speech is actual. It is a way in which
speech dwells, but not as a mere privation waiting upon revelation and
the bringing forth of meaning. Silence understood as the absence of
speech in and of itself is invested with meaning. The other, for example, interrogates me with a question I cannot answer. In my speech-
lessness I discover who I am. "I am like a dumb man who cannot open
his mouth. I behave like a man who cannot hear and whose tongue
offers no defense."[314] The Psalmist, in likening himself to a deaf man,
recognizes that he is, in fact, one who does speak. The deaf are silent;
they cannot *hear*. The Psalmist, on the other hand, expresses an
awareness of the unnoticed absence of speech.

Speech manifests itself as absence only for one who dwells already in the expectation of speech. Silence may appear as speech that
is unable, unwilling, or lacking the necessity to become expressed
speech. Yet, even the pauses within speech that cannot be registered
on any devices that measure noticeable sound are not concessions to
the imperfection of speech but rather enable its very possibility. If
silence is something that can be heard, then we are peculiarly mindful
of its distinguishable appearances as, for example, when we speak of a

long, painful silence — or when we notice the still quiet of early morning that precedes the bustle of everyday activity. The pauses within living speech, on the other hand, are almost always unnoticed just because of the omnipresence of their occurences. Neither the speaker nor the hearer falls out of being at those ever repeated moments in discourse when they are between spoken words. The temporality of speech, what occurs within speech as it unfolds from future to past to present, discloses the presence of rest, transition, and the ingathering of meaning that, in stilling the upsurge of speech, permits its expression into distinguishable units. The occasion of looking for a missing word, the right word, the words unspoken and longed for are all occasions in which the phenomenon of absence informs the content of speech.

The absence of speech may become the incarnation of silence. For example, the previously unnoticed stillness in which I dwell alone is reckoned by me as silence only retrospectively after the other has made his appearance in the midst of shared discourse. The silence that occurs at the end of a conversation is different in kind from the silence that precedes discourse and is found within it. Here Heidegger's distinction between time, as the horizon within which Being manifests itself, and temporality is useful. The very capacity for meaningful units of speech to appear depends upon the capacity of speech to withhold itself, to be delimited, in order that it might become. How can there be sentences unless the grammar of living speech can be rendered divisible? Without the pauses that occur between statements, there could be only one run-on sentence heard from the beginning of time until the end. This same capacity of language to render itself divisible makes it possible for us to distinguish the appearances of individual words and utterances. But remarkably we are taught everything about language and speech, the science of linguistics, the rules for using language properly, the science of statements logic, yet most of the time we dwell in the absence of speech about which we speak little and understand less.

Friendship demands an acquaintance with the meaning of absence. To be absent is the face which friendship wears when the friend is not near at hand. If the absent friend cannot beacon his absence toward the present, there can be no "friends", only "momentary" acquaintances.

Fidelity demands a knowledge of the meaning of absence. Withholding oneself in the face of the present that entreats acquiescence is a necessary precondition for faithfulness to the absent one. Betrayal begins with 'ressentiment' against the absent friend, the secret declaration that he is nonexistent.

To dwell in the absence of justice, where justice is postponed, without succumbing, therefore, to a belief in its nonexistence, is a necessary precondition grounding the possibility of any ethical life. The universalizability of justice depends upon the capacity of reckoning with all of the absent others, where distance is a function of spatial separation or the absence of temporal proximity. Otherwise, what is unjust can manifest itself only as the gratuitious suffering inflicted upon myself, at this present moment. Here, we should be forced to conclude, along with Dostoevsky's man from the underground, that the aspiration for justice lives within the circle of 'ressentiment'.

Heidegger is claiming that just as that which is unsaid and remains to be said steers the direction of living speech from out of the absent future, the phenomenon of absence itself enables Being to withhold itself, and therefore to unfold as time. The act of devaluing the meaning of absence, the reduction of absence to nothingness, serves to represent Being as that which appears only in the momentary "now". It governs the interpretation of the static concept of temporality which leads inevitably to the rancor against time. It is the 'ressentiment' against absence, therefore, that serves as the ultimate ontological ground of the rancor against time.

The ground has now been prepared for resolving the riddle Nietzsche posed in anticipation of the solution to the rancor against time: "to breed an animal that *has the right to make promises* — is not this the paradoxical task that nature has set itself in the case of man? is it not the real problem regarding man?"[315]

To promise is the shape of the perfect structural deed. To promise is to bind the absent deed to the word spoken in the present. It represents the existential triumph over the rancor against time. To make good on the word spoken is to remain faithful to a two-fold absence: that of the being I am to become and that of the other, for whom I shall become past and deed. In the act of promising I bind together the ecstatic phases of human temporality, and become one.

To promise is the *it* of which Heidegger speaks, the ontological act of *Appropriation* whereby Being binds itself to man. *It* withholds itself as absence and, thereby, offers the gift of presence. To be absent is a moment of the promise that, by engendering the becoming of presence, permits the emergence of the appearance of beings. The founding premise of the circle of 'ressentiment' is revalued, transformed, and taken within the ontological first premise, that to be is to promise.

V. CONCLUSION

Surfacing the submerged phenomenon of 'ressentiment' from its subterranean depths in human existence demands a new accountability on
the part of contemporary philosophy for the question concerning the
relation of Being to meaning. The struggle against 'ressentiment' in-
volves philosophy in a re-examination of its essential project — the
wresting of meaning out of that which *is*. The mode of being of
'ressentiment' is to decide for nothingness over Being. It is the fundamental thematic thrust characterizing the decisionlessness of modern
existence. The phenomenon of 'ressentiment' disclosed in the full
ontological reach of its implications opens for philosophical questioning the credibility of the enterprise of philosophy by demanding an
account of how it is possible that the transient character of being
human permits man to care about anything at all.

Dostoevsky has described man wrestling with the problem of
decisionlessness, the struggle against *becoming* a self in time against
the tyranny of time frozen in the Crystal Palace. The man from underground self-consciously imposes the burden of suffering upon himself
so as at least to remain awake to the promise of meaning where none
could be found or created. Dostoevsky refused to put his imprimatur
on the denial of the self-defining human aspiration to coerce meaning
from all the forces threatening its destruction. He exposed the price
to be paid for the decision that rejects responsibility of man's accountability to Being. He makes evident the fundamental strategy of
'ressentiment' by which man seeks a system of hideouts within which
to seek refuge from the arduous task of living in the absence of
conviction. The maxim by which the underground man lives — to be
in the absence of self-deception — presumes the existence, however
remote, of authentic understanding that promises man the prospect
of redeeming a life fated to error, imperfection, guilt, and finitude.

Scheler brilliantly fastened on the mode of 'ressentiment' that
flees from the factical shape of the present. He traced through the
movement whereby denial originates in the face of intuitively reckoned self-apprehension and eventuates in the devaluation of an experienced hierarchy, that is, however, taken by him to be the natural
aristocracy of the social order. As he has exposed the surface appear-

ances of 'ressentiment' in the modern industrial world, Scheler's description has resubmerged the ontological dimension of Nietzsche's questioning. Scheler's phenomenology cannot explain the conditions which engendered the Crystal Palace, nor its reflected inversion, the underground.

Scheler's efforts in the direction of a resolution provide surcease from the suffering experienced by modern man as gratuitous and unwarranted, and thus yielding 'ressentiment', only by collapsing the distinction between the meaningful and the meaningless appearances of human agony.

The verticality which Scheler wishes to preserve, as belonging, by nature, to the community of mortals, is eradicated in a stroke. Scheler's resolution of the problem, the doctrine of agapistic love, as rendered by him, gains a pyrrhic victory at each of the intervals of time by treating all of the others as though they were nonexistent. His solution works only in the realm of formal definition, in which meaning captures Being, by devaluing historicity. He cannot, therefore, explain how each epoch is appropriated by the Being of meaning, and takes its unique stance towards the perennial challenge posed by 'ressentiment'.

The reflection of Nietzsche probed the metaphysical roots of philosophical 'ressentiment' from which has flowered the appearance of all the many concealed ways in which man has hidden the nothingness of Being from himself. Nietzsche offered a profound philosophic account of those conditions which have combined to engender the appearance of the underground itself. The substitution of Nietzsche's meditation on the rancor against time for Dostoevsky's description of the man of 'ressentiment' demonstrates how Being itself has been reckoned and determined out of the spirit of revenge. Dostoevsky's man from underground glimpses the appearances of a life that has enjoined reason to existential madness and has imposed the pseudo-decision for nothingness, negation and death upon the promise that binds absent understanding to the revealed truth of the present.

The full maturation of human possibility appears, for Nietzsche, with the advent of the liberation of man from all falsified relations to nonexistent absolutes. The death of meaning in the night of nihilism forces the inner illumination that reveals how man stands related to time reckoned out of the spirit of revenge. The understanding of the inner dynamic of how man comprehends in advance of the agony of death, the meaning of his own perishing mirrored in each passing moment, simultaneously explains the devaluation of becoming and offers the prospect of the revaluation of what it means for man to be.

The existential questioning concerning the value and meaning of all particular and regional preoccupations forces a re-thinking of the essential vocation of man's enduring work, his will-to-meaning. Man's fatedness to historicity, suffering, longing, and error may be reconceived and revalued if the fundamental rancor against time is met cleanly and the ever-present 'ressentiment'-laden valuation of the Being of time is resisted. But, what eternally recurs is not the self-same present, as Nietzsche wrongly concludes — thus assisting in covering over the profundity and dynamic relevance of his own questioning. Rather, it is the structure of relatedness between this inescapable questioning — the demand for resolution — the simultaneous prospect of response and the virtual absence of resolution. What recurs on Nietzsche's account is not the end of 'ressentiment', but the devaluation of what it means to care about meaning and the question of how the Being of time can engender such an existence for the being quickened by the recognition of what it means to be finite.

Heidegger has established a philosophical foundation for demonstrating the possibility of a life that can be lived above ground without succumbing to the delusion that the frozen time symbolized by the palace of crystal is exhaustive of human promise. The time of Being is *ec-static* temporality, time that is out of joint with itself.

It is open to the determination of the fragile human will to determine how it will stand with respect to its own mortality. The concept of static time depends, as Heidegger has shown, upon the ontologically prior reality of lived-time. Something remarkable has been achieved, a way of reckoning with the abiding presence of the phases of time, disestablishing the ground of the rancor against time and establishing an horizon within which thought can move in the direction of overcoming the 'ressentiment' against the Being of time.

Now it begins to be possible to understand how Being gives itself as the event of time. To *be-come* is a philosophically meaningful expression only if Being offers itself in the shape of Promise.

The phenomenology of absence is a gate that opens onto the phenomenon of Promise. The same four-fold movement must be repeated if we are to begin to understand how it already informs the life of lived-experience, if we try to understand its eidetic structures, and the dynamic of the binding of the absent deed to the word spoken in the present — the concrete way in which the good opens to man in time.

A hermeneutical circle of promise must subtend and ground the one that depicts the structures of 'ressentiment'. Nietzsche's historicity and ontology of 'ressentiment', brilliant, one-sided, profound, must be re-animated within the ontology of promise. A more balanced reflection of the way Being has and does appear to thought can then be offered. Heidegger's own fundamental ontology needs to be rethought in the light of his later discovery. How does 'Dasein' comprehend and confirm the infinite promise of the finite other?

VI. FOOTNOTES

[1] Max Scheler, Ressentiment, trans. William W. Holdheim, ed. Lewis A. Coser (New York: The Free Press of Glencoe, 1961), p. 43.

[2] Translation from the French: Larousse de Poche, eighth printing (New York: Washington Square Press, 1941), p. 339: "n.m., Souvenir d'une offense, d'un manque d'egards, avec intention de vengeance".

[3] Ressentiment, p. 39.

[4] Random House College Edition Dictionary, ed. (Editor-in-chief) Lawrence Urdang and (Managing Editor) Stuart Berg Flexner (New York: Random House, 1968).

[5] Friedrich Nietzsche, On the Genealogy of Morals trans. Walter Kaufmann and R. J. Hollingdale (New York: Vintage Books, Random House, 1967. See 'Third Essay', Aphorism 15 on p. 127 (Author's emphasis).

[6] Martin Heidegger, What is Called Thinking?, trans. Fred D. Wieck and J. Glenn Gray (New York: Harper and Row, 1968).

[7] Nietzsche, "Letter to Overbeck, February 23, 1887". In: The Portable Nietzsche, ed. Walter Kaufmann (New York: Viking Press, 1954), p. 454.

[8] See: Existentialism from Dostoevsky to Sartre, ed. Walter Kaufmann (New York: World Publishing, Time Mirror, 1956), p. 52—82, an anthology of existential writings, containing only Part I of the 'Notes from the Underground'; see also: Existentialism, ed. by Robert C. Solomon (New York: Random House, 1974), p. 32—42; Konstantin Mochulsky, Dostoevsky, trans. Michael A. Minihan (Princeton, New Jersey: Princeton University Press, 1971), p. 242—270. In an exhaustive survey cataloguing critical commentary on Dostoevsky, Rene Wellek, states in 'Dostoevsky: A Collection of Critical Essays' (Englewood Cliffs: Prentice-Hall, 1962), p. 6: "Mochulsky meticulously interprets figures, scenes, and meanings actually present in the novels." Yet Mochulsky's twenty-eight page essay on the 'Notes' includes only three pages on Part II (pages 257—260). The comments of N. Berdyaev, V. Ivanov, and A. Gide are even more sparse. Geoffrey Clive's 'The Romantic Enlightenment' (Westport, Conn.: Greenwood Press, 1960), p. 96—150, especially p. 96—132, is a notable exception in two respects: 1) Clive makes perceptive remarks throughout on Part II even if he is unconcerned with the relation between Parts I and II; 2) his commentary on the 'Notes' is the only sustained philosophical investigation into the content of the 'Notes'. Its main strength is also its most constraining weakness. Clive superimposes Kierkegaardian categories upon Dostoevsky's presentation in which the latter is more often than not understood as expressing in a groping way the conceptual truths of the former.

[9] Plato, Apology, 22 A-C.

[10] Fyodor Dostoevsky, Notes from the Underground, trans. Constance Garnett (New York: Vintage Press, Vintage Russian Library, 1968), p. 179.

[11] Ibid., p. 200.

[12] Ibid, pp. 221—28.

[13] Ibid., pp. 231—52.

[14] Ibid., pp. 252—96.

[15] Albert Camus, The Myth of Sisyphus and Other Essays, trans. Justin O' Brien (New York: Random House, Vintage Press, 1955).

[16] Walter Kaufmann, ed., Existentialism from Dostoevsky to Sartre (New York: World Publishing, Time Mirror, 1956), p. 312.

[17] Myth of Sisyphus, p. 90.

[18] Ibid., p. 89.

[19] Ibid., p. 90.

[20] Ibid., p. 89.

[21] Ibid., p. 89—90.

[22] See Homer's: The Odyssey, Book II, lines 600—610.

[23] As stated by Protagoras of Abdera: "From 'Truth' or 'Refutory Arguments'." "Of all things the measure is man, of the things that are, that they are and of the things that are not, that they are not." See Diels's: Ancilla to the Pre-Socratic Philosophers, trans. Kathleen Freeman (Cambridge, Mass.: Harvard University Press, 1971), p. 125.

[24] Myth of Sisyphus, p. 90.

[25] Ibid.

[26] Ibid., p. 91.

[27] Aristotle, Nicomachean Ethics, Book I, Chapter 7, in: The Basic Works of Aristotle, ed. Richard McKeon (New York: Random House, 1941), p. 943.

[28] Myth of Sisyphus, p. 89.

[29] Ibid., p. 90.

[30] Ibid.

[31] Ibid., p. 91.

[32] See William Shakespeare, Macbeth in: The Complete Signet Classic Shakespeare, ed. Sylvan Barnet, p. 1259: "I, 'gin to be aweary of the sun/And wish th' estate o' th' world were now undone."

[33] Notes from the Underground, p. 188—89.

[34] Ibid., p. 189.

[35] Ibid., p. 197.

[36] Ibid.

[37] Ibid., p. 200.

[38] Ibid.

[39] Ibid., p. 192.

[40] Ibid.

[41] Ibid.

[42] See especially Plato, 'Symposium', 200A—212C, trans. Michael Joyce, in: The Collected Dialogues of Plato (Princeton: Princeton University Press, 2nd printing, 1963), pp. 552—563.

[43] Notes, p. 224.

[44] Ibid., p. 225.

[45] Ibid., p. 200.

[46] Ibid., p. 201.

[47] Ibid., p. 180.

[48] Ibid.

[49] Ibid., p. 295.

[50] Ibid., p. 181.

[51] Ibid., p. 296.

[52] Friedrich Nietzsche, On the Genealogy of Morals (New York: Random House, Vintage Press, 1967), p. 127 (Author's emphasis).

[53] Dostoevsky, Brothers Karamazov, trans. Constance Garnett (New York: Vintage Press, Vintage Russian Library, 1968), p. 758.

[54] Notes, p. 181 (Author's emphasis).

[55] Ibid., p. 179.

[56] Max Scheler, Ressentiment, ed. Lewis A. Coser, trans. William W. Holdeim (Free Press of Glencoe, 1961). See "Prefatory Remarks", p. 34.

[57] Ibid., p. 37.

[58] Ibid.

[59] Ibid. In Footnote I, 'Ressentiment', Scheler refers to Jaspers's book 'Allgemeine Psycholpathologie' (Berlin, 1913) in which is distinguished the "difference between causal connections (*Kausalzusammenhänge*) and understandable context (*Verständniszusammenhänge*) in mental life".

[60] Ibid., p. 38.

[61] Ibid.

[62] Ibid.

[63] Ibid.

[64] Ibid.

[65] Ibid.

[66] Ibid., p. 39.

[67] Ibid. (Author's emphasis).

[68] Ibid., p. 45 (Author's emphasis).

[69] Ibid., p. 45—46.

[70] Ibid., p. 46.

[71] Ibid. (My emphasis).

[72] Ibid.

[73] Ibid.

[74] Ibid.

[75] Ibid., p. 47.

[76] Ibid.

[77] Ibid.

[78] See the controlling place in the concept of the material a priori in Scheler's most famous work, 'Der Formalismus in der Ethik und die materiale Wertetik', 2 volumes (Halle, 1913—1916).

[79] Ressentiment, p. 47.

[80] Ibid.

[81] Ibid.

[82] Ibid., p. 46.

[83] Ibid., p. 48.

[84] Ibid., p. 47.

[85] Ibid., p. 48.

[86] Ibid., p. 49.

[87] Ibid.

[88] Ibid.

[89] Ibid.

[90] Ibid.

[91] Ibid. (Author's emphasis).

[92] Martin Heidegger, Being and Time, trans. John Macquarrie and Edward Robinson (London: SMC Press, 1962). See Div. II, Sec. 37.

[93] Being and Time, Div. I, Int. II, p. 62.

[94] Ibid. According to Nietzsche's analysis, we shall see, corresponding to the primary injury occasioning the possible origin of the 'ressentiment', is man's experience of time's passage.

[95] Scheler's phenomenology assumes the "givenness" of human suffering.

[96] See Aristotle's 'Rhetoric', Book II, Ch. 9 in: The Basic Works of Aristotle, ed. Richard McKeon (New York: Random House, 1941), p. 1399: "If you are pained by the unmerited distress of others, you will be pleased or at least not pained by their merited distress." Why? Aristotle simply does not explain.

[97] It is first directed at Agememnon when the latter has robbed him of his prize, Briseis. The sadness that accompanies this loss of face and possession grounds the appearance of the anger directed towards Agamemnon. The wrath directed against Hector and the Trojans is prepared for by his sorrowing over the death of his beloved Patroclus. Both of these concrete expressions of anger are in turn prefigured by the sense of loss and are a reflection of the anger embodied in the knowledge that he must die prematurely to gain honor and glory.

Subsequent to the break with Agamemnon, Achilles suffers from resentment. He sulks with the Myrmidons throughout most of the 'Iliad', grieving over his loss of honor. Resentment turns into the desire for revenge, to see the Greeks punished until they come to appreciate the absence of their greatest warrior.

Rancor originates when the desire for revenge is concealed, when in the case of Achilles, he denies to himself in the presence of his friends his desire to see the Greeks suffer. The wrath of Achilles moving toward 'ressentiment' breaks out of the self-perpetuating circle upon hearing the news of the death of Patroclus.

[98] Ressentiment, p. 53.

[99] Ibid., p. 52.

[100] Ibid.

[101] Ibid., p. 48.

[102] Ibid.

[103] Ibid., p. 50 (Author's emphasis).

[104] Ibid., p. pp. 60—61.

[105] Ibid., p. 65.

[106] Ibid.

[107] Ibid., p. 61.

[108] Ibid., p. 61—62 (Author's emphasis).

[109] Ibid., p. 66.

[110] See: Friedrich Nietzsche, On the Genealogy of Morals, trans. Walter Kaufmann and R. J. Hollingdale (New York: Random House, Vintage Press, 1967).

[111] Ressentiment, pp. 66—67.

[112] Ibid., p. 67.

[113] Ibid.

[114] Ibid., p. 64.

[115] Ibid.

[116] Ibid.

[117] Ibid.

[118] Ibid., p. 62.

[119] Ibid., p. 64.

[120] Ibid., p. 57.

[121] Ibid., p. 67.

[122] Ibid. (Author's emphasis).

[123] Ibid., p. 62 (Author's emphasis).

[124] Ibid., p. 63.

[125] Ibid., pp. 63—64.

[126] Ibid., p. 53 (My emphasis).

[127] Ibid.

[128] Ibid.

[129] Ibid., p. 50.

[130] Ibid., p. 50—51.

[131] Ibid., p. 50.

[132] Ibid., p. 66.

[133] Ibid., p. 56.

[134] Ibid., pp. 56—57 (Author's emphasis).

[135] Ibid., see especially p. 84: ". . . in Greek eyes the whole phenomenon of 'love' belongs to the domain of the senses. It is a form of 'desire', or 'need', etc., which is foreign to the most perfect form of being."

". . . the most perfect form of being cannot know 'aspiration' or 'need' . . ."

[136] Ibid.

[137] Ibid.

[138] Ibid.

[139] Scheler's conception of the Greek concept of love does not permit us, however, to explain why it is that Socrates desires to share the endeavor of philosophy with others to whom he is clearly superior in wisdom and understanding. Why does the philosopher return to the cave of ignorance having once stood in the light of knowledge, and without any apparent gain to be derived from his descent? Of course, it could be argued that he is merely helping to bring about a world safe for the activity of philosophy in which the creation of the just state will mean that the danger that accompanies the pursuit of wisdom will be diminished. Moreover, Scheler could point out that the lover of wisdom is moved by the appearances that lead to wisdom, thus substantiating his case that even in the person of Socrates, the lover, he is moved by the beloved. Still, it is misleading to say, as Scheler does in the case of Greek love, that it is "only a road to something else, a *'methodos'*." Scheler can make this assertion again if, and only if, 'eros' is incapable of transformation, and if it can be proved by him that love exists of a superior sort that does not move towards the object of its intention.

[140] Plato, 'Symposium', 200e, in: The Collected Dialogues of Plato, ed. Edith Hamilton and Huntington Cairns, (Princeton: Princeton University Press for Bollingen Foundation, 1963).

[141] Ressentiment, pp. 84—85.

[142] Ibid., p. 85 (Author's emphasis).

[143] Ibid.

[144] Ibid., p. 86—87.

[145] Book of Genesis, (The Holy Scriptures according to the Masoretic text), p. 4.

[146] Plato, Euthyphro, trans. H. N. Fowler (Cambridge: Harvard University Press, 1960. See lines 9e—10a.

[147] Ressentiment, pp. 94—95 (author's emphasis). It should be noted that the God of Plotinus is not personal, although the emanationist's theory of creation derives from 'Enneads'. See especially 'Enneads', VI.

[148] Ibid., p. 87 (Author's emphasis).

[149] One contrast between the speeches of Aristophanes and that of Socrates refers to different kinds of 'needs' and does not, therefore, make the distinction clear.

[150] Emmanuel Levinas, Totality and Infinity, trans. Alphonso Lingis (Pittsburgh, Pa.: Duquesne University Press, 1969), p. 34.

[151] Ressentiment, p. 87 (Author's emphasis).

[152] See G. E. Moore, Principal Ethica, Ch. I, # 6, anthologized and edited by Sellers and Hospers (New York: Meredith Corporation, 1970).

[153] Ressentiment, p. 94 (Author's emphasis).

[154] Ibid.

[155] Ibid.

[156] Totality and Infinity, pp. 257—57 (Author's emphasis).

[157] Ressentiment, p. 91 (Author's emphasis).

[158] Ibid., p. 91—92.

[159] Ibid., p. 96 (Author's emphasis).

[160] Ibid., p. 100—101 (Author's emphasis).

[161] See ibid., p. 109.

[162] See Psalm 90, line 12: "Teach us to number our days that we may get us a heart of wisdom."

[163] Ressentiment, pp. 144—45.

[164] 'Philosophy in the Tragic Age of the Greeks' [Die Philosophie im tragischen Zeitalter der Griechen], was written during the period in which was published 'The Birth of Tragedy' [Die Geburt der Tragädie aus dem Geiste der Musik] (1872).

[165] Friedrich Nietzsche, Philosophy in the Tragic Age of the Greeks, trans. Mary Ann Cowan (Chicago: Henry Regnery Co., 1962), p. 45. Corresponding to the classical text of the Anaximander fragment is the following transliteration: "ex on de ē génesís esti tois oúsi kai tēn phthoran eís taúta gínesthai kata to chreón; didonai gar autà diken kai tisin allēlois tes adikías kata tēn tou chrónov taxín.

[166] Ibid., p. 48.

[167] Ibid.

[168] Ibid., p. 45.

[169] Ibid., p. 48.

[170] Ibid.

[171] Friedrich Nietzsche, The Use and Abuse of History, (2nd ed.) trans. Adrian Collins (Indianapolis: Liberal Arts Press of Bobbs-Merill Co., 1957), p. 12.

[172] Ibid., p. 21.

[173] Ibid., p. 40 (Author's emphasis).

[174] Ibid., p. 11.

[175] Martin Heidegger, Being and Time, trans. John Macquarrie and Edward Robinson (London: SMC Press, 1962). See Div. V (Temporality and Historicality), Sec. 72, 376, p. 428 (Author's emphasis).

[176] Tragic Age of the Greeks, p. 48.

[177] Nietzsche, Twilight of the Idols, trans. Walter Kaufmann, in: The Portable Nietzsche, ed. Walter Kaufmann (New York: Viking Press, 1954). See 'The Problem of Socrates', Aphorism I, p. 473.

[178] Ibid.

[179] Ibid.

[180] Ibid., p. 474 (Author's emphasis).

[181] Ibid.

[182] How can Nietzsche himself make a judgment on the given value of life if such judgments are claimed to be impossible? This is a specific instance of the general tendency of Nietzsche to violate the principle of noncontradiction, knowingly, in order to polemicize a position.

[183] Twilight of the Idols, Aphorism 5, p. 476 (Author's emphasis).

[184] Ibid.

[185] Ibid.

[186] Ibid., Aphorism 4, p. 474.

[187] Ibid.

[188] Ibid., Aphorism 3, p. 474. Nietzsche does not trouble to make Aristotle's distinction between ugliness that a man can be blamed for by living a life of vice and inhereited ugliness — no doubt he would see such a distinction as itself the result of decline.

[189] Ibid., Aphorism 7, p. 476 (Author's emphasis).

[190] Ibid., Aphorism 8, p. 477.

[191] Ibid., Aphorism 9, p. 477 (Author's emphasis).

[192] Ibid. (Author's emphasis).

[193] Ibid.

[194] Ibid. (Author's emphasis).

[195] Ibid. (Author's emphasis).

[196] Ibid. (Author's emphasis).

[197] Ibid.

[198] It is not by accident that Homer depicts all of the major figures of the 'Iliad' as beautiful in outward form.

[199] Ibid., Aphorism 10, p. 478 (Author's emphasis).

[200] Ibid. (Author's emphasis).

[201] Nietzsche, The Birth of Tragedy, trans. Walter Kaufmann (New York: Random House, 1967); Sec. 15, p. 92—96 (Author's emphasis).

[202] Ibid., p. 96 (Author's emphasis).

[203] Ibid., Sec. 3, p. 43.

[204] Twilight of the Idols, "The Problem of Socrates", Aphorism 11, p. 478 (Author's emphasis).

[205] Ibid., Aphorism 12, p. 479 (Author's emphasis).

[206] Ibid., "Reason in Philosophy", Aphorsim 2, p. 480.

[207] Ibid., Aphorism 1, pp. 479—80 (Author's emphasis).

[208] Ibid., Aphorism 2, p. 480.

[209] Ibid., p. 481.

[210] Ibid.

[211] The Book of John: 14:6 in: the New English Bible (New York: Oxford University Press, 1971).

[212] Nietzsche, On the Genealogy of Morals, trans. Walter Kaufmann and R. J. Hollingdale (New York: Random House, Vintage Press, 1967). Note especially the Second Essay, Section 22, p. 93 (Author's emphasis).

[213] Twilight of the Idols, "Reason In Philosophy", Aphorism 6, p. 484.

[214] Ibid. See "How the 'True World' Finally Became A Fable: The History of an Error", p. 485.

[215] See: Joan Stambaugh, Nietzsche's Thought of Eternal Return (Baltimore and London: John Hopkins University Press, 1972). Stambaugh misses the dialectical thrust of Nietzsche's capsule summary of the history of philosophy. She fails to recognize that it is through the radicalization of the error of metaphysics that Nietzsche locates an aperture in being that prepares the advent of the new understanding of the relation of appearance to reality.

[216] Twilight of the Idols, "How the 'True World' Finally Became a Fable", p. 485 (Author's emphasis).

[217] Nietzsche has in mind the emerging philosophical positivism of a Mach which is later to culminate in Wittgenstein's 'Tractatus — Logico — Philosophicus' and A. J. Ayer's 'Language, Truth, and Logic'.

[218] Twilight of the Idols, p. 485—86 (Author's emphasis).

[219] Ibid., p. 486 (Author's emphasis).

[220] Ibid., p. 34.

[221] Whether Nietzsche believed that such criteriological distinctions "between appearances and reality, becoming and being, illusion and truth" could ever be drawn — as Magnus assumes, is a suitable subject of inquiry — is discussed in: Bernd Magnus, Heidegger's Metahistory of Philosophy (The Hague: Martinus Nijhoff, 1970).

[222] Twilight of the Idols, "How the 'True World' Became . . .", p. 486.

[223] Nietzsche, Thus Spake Zarathustra, in: The Portable Nietzsche. See especially Part II, "On Redemption", p. 251.

[224] Ibid.

[225] Ibid., p. 251—52 (Author's emphasis). See also: Heidegger, What Is Called Thinking?, trans. Fred Wieck and J. Glenn Gray (New York: Harper and Row, 1968).

[226] Zarathustra, p. 252.

[227] Ibid., Part I, "Zarathustra's Prologue", Sec. 4, pp. 126—28 (Author's emphasis).

[228] What Is Called Thinking?, p. 4 (Author's emphasis).

[229] Zarathustra, Part II, "On Redemption", p. 252.

[230] What Is Called Thinking?, p. 4.

[231] Zarathustra, p. 252—53.

[232] The position advanced by Eryximachus is rejected out of hand by Plato. See Plato's 'Symposium'.

[233] Zarathustra, Part I, "Zarathustra's Prologue', Sec. 5, p. 129 (Author's emphasis).

[234] Twilight of the Idols, p. 471 (no. 31).

[235] Zarathustra, Part II, "On the Pitying", p. 200.

[236] Ibid., Part II, "On Redemption", p. 250—51 (Author's emphasis).

[237] Ibid., p. 251.

[238] Ibid., Part II, "On the Tarantulas", p. 211 (Author's emphasis).

[239] Nietzsche, "Ecce Homo" in: The Basic Writings of Nietzsche, trans. and ed. Walter Kaufmann (New York: Random House, 1968), p. 751.

[240] Zarathustra, Part III, "The Convalescent", p. 332 (Author's emphasis).

[241] Nietzsche, The Will to Power, trans. Walter Kaufmann and R. J. Hollingdale (New York: Random House, Vintage Press, 1968), # 617, p. 330 (Author's emphasis).

Bernd Magnus concludes his brilliant refutation of Nietzsche's theory of the eternal return as a cosmological formulation by commenting that: "The empirical arguments for eternal recurrence are a tissue of ambiguity". [Magnus, "Nietzsche's Eternalistic Counter-Myth", Review of Metaphysics: Vol. 26, (June 1973).] Magnus argues that Nietzsche is incorrect in inferring that a finite sum of energy implies a finite number of energy states. Drawing upon the four essential features of Nietzsche's Cosmological Formulation of the Eternal Recurrence argument, Magnus asserts that Nietzsche's improper inference weakens his arguments fatally. The four essential features of the cosmological formulation of the eternal return theory Magnus locates as follows:

1) Space is finite
2) Energy is finite
3) Time is infinite
4) No terminal state in the configuration of energy has ever been reached.

The conclusion which Nietzsche draws from the cumulative weight of these four premises is that in an infinite time, a finite number of energy configurations will recur. Nietzsche specifies in the crucial passage from the "Nachlass" that "Up to this moment an infinity has passed; i.e., all possible developments have already come to pass" (Nachlass XII). If this highly controversial assumption is allowed to pass as true within the context of the other four equally assailable assumptions, then we are forced to conclude, with Magnus, that for Nietzsche the possible world must be reducible to the actual world — in fact, they are identical. Again, this is already granting Nietzsche his most improbable inference that from (2) above a finite amount of enery, one can deduce a finite amount of energy configurations or states.

But if we accept such a Leibnizian reduction of the possible to the actual then, as Magnus points out, there is yet lacking the precondition to establish the possibility or, more precisely, the actual advent of novelty and, hence, the establishment of a necessary condition for the world's recurring at all is found wanting. On the other hand, if we accept the fact that Nietzsche requires the concept of logical possibility in order to explain the genesis of each "new" beginning which would presumably be restored to its original career, then a problem arises regarding the identity of indiscernibles. On this interpretation, actual energy states are not the only possible ones. Magnus illustrates this horn of the dilemma by picturing the case of someone other than myself, who is exactly like me in all observable respects and who either acted or refrained from acting in an identical manner at an identical time (p. 606). We should have to conclude that the other and I either were the same person, in which case we should have to abandon the sense bestowed by the pronominal "I". Or, if we wish to preserve the meaning of this first person utterance, then we should have to fault Nietzsche for lacking a concept of logical possibility which would permit the virtue of the enabling conditions of spatial and temporal location. Magnus is on safe ground in concluding that: "Nietzsche needs the concept of logical possibility on the one hand, while needing to reject its implications on the other".

[242] Zarathustra, Part III, Sec. 2, "On the Vision and the Riddle", pp. 269—70.

[243] Ibid., p. 270 (Author's emphasis).

[244] Ibid.

[245] See: What Is Called Thinking?, p. 106.

[246] Zarathustra, Part II, "On the Soothsayers", p. 245.

[247] Ibid.

[248] Ibid., Part III, "The Convalescent", Sec. 1, p. 328.

[249] Ibid.

[250] Ibid.

[251] Ibid., p. 329.

[252] Twilight of the Idols, "Reason In Philosophy", Aphorism 5, p. 483.

[253] Zarathustra, Part III, "The Convalescent", Aphorism 2, pp. 329—30.

[254] Friedrich Nietzsche, Genealogy of Morals, transl. Francis Golffing (Doubleday & Co., New York, 1956), "Second Essay", Aphorism 1, p. 57 (My emphasis).

[255] Zarathustra, Part I, see "On the Child and Marriage".

[256] Ibid., Part II, "On the Tarantulas", p. 214.

He will transvalue the meaning of human equality. Unlike Scheler who finds the spirit of revenge in every movement that attempts to reposition the hierarchy of men and excellences "given" by nature, that which is "overman" for Nietzsche summons forth the ontological self-overcoming on the part of man himself.

Nietzsche's point of departure in reflecting on the desire for equality expressed in the section "On Tarantulas" is identical with Scheler's conclusion: "Thus I speak to you in a parable — you who make souls whirl, you preachers of *equality*. To me you are tarantulas and secretely vengeful . . . the tyramomania of impotence clamors thus out of your for equality. Your most secret ambitions to be tyrants thus showed themselves in words of virtue. Aggrieved conceit, repressed envy — perhaps the conceit and envy of your fathers — erupt from you as a flame and as the frenzy of revenge. . . . I do not wish to be mixed up and confused with these preachers of equality. For, to *me* justice speaks thus: "Men are not equal! What would my love of the overman be if I spoke otherwise? (Thus Spake Zarathustra, pp. 211—13, Author's emphasis).

Nietzsche's reflection, however, does not stop here. It is not wedded to a doctrine that is either politically reactionary or revolutionary. Certainly, it is not intended to shore up the hierarchy of values exemplifed in the age of nihilism. It is not committed, with Scheler, to viewing the French revolution as sublime creation of the spirit of revenge and the Crusades as triumph of eternal truths. It offers a reflection on life that "wants to build itself up into the heights with pillars and steps . . . Life wants to climb and to overcome itself climbing" (Zarathustra, p. 219).

Nietzsche's reflection on equality is not content to expose the holes in which the tarantulas reside. Zarathustra prepares the way for what is overman when the spirit of revenge informs all previous struggles for equality which will be incorporated and transcended: "And behold, my friends: here where the tarantula has its hole, the ruins of ancient temples rise; behold it with enlightened eyes! Verily, the man who once piled his thoughts to the sky in these stones — he, like the wisest, knew the secret of all life. That struggle and inequality are present even in beauty, and also war, power and more power: that is what he teaches here in the plainest parable. How divinely vault and arches break through each other in a wrestling match; how they strive against each other with light and shade, the godlike strivers — with such assurance and beauty — with such assurance and beauty let us be enemies too, my friends! *Let us strive against each other like gods*." (Zarathustra, p. 213—214, Author's emphasis).

[257] Ibid., Part III, "The Convalescent", p. 329.

[258] Ibid., Part I, "On the Friend", p. 168 (Author's emphasis).

[259] See: Kirk and Raven, The Presocratic Philosophers (Cambridge: Cambridge University Press, 1971), pp. 196—98, for an in-depth discussion on the references made to this Heraclitean fragment in Greek philosophical texts.

[260] Paul Tillich, The Courage To Be (New Haven, Conn.: Yale University Press, 1952), p. 28.

[261] Note Heidegger in 'Being and Time', Div. II, page 475: "The sequence of 'nows' is taken as something that is somehow present-at-hand, for it even moves 'into time'. ... In *every* 'now' the 'now' is now and therefore it constantly has presence *as something selfsame*, even though in every 'now' another may be vanishing as it comes along. Yet as *this* thing which changes, it simultaneously shows its own constant presence. Thus even Plato, who directed his glance in this manner at time as a sequence of 'nows' arising and passing away, had to call time 'the image of eternity'.* But he decided to make a kind of moving image of the eternal; and while setting the heavens in order, he made an eternal image, moving according to number — an image of eternity which abides in oneness. It is to this image that we have given the name of 'time'."
*See Plato, Timaeus, 37d.

[262] Martin Heidegger, Being and Time, trans. John Macquarrie and Edward Robinson (London: SCM Press), 1962. See "Preface", untitled page (Author's emphasis).

[263] See: Being and Time, Div. II, Sec. 24, p. 46, where Heidegger discusses Descartes' failure to determine "the meaning of the Being of the 'sum'."

[264] See: Being and Time, Div. I. 1, Sec. 42, p. 67: "We are ourselves the entities to be analysed. The Being of any such entity is *in each case mine*. These entities, in the Being, comport themselves towards their Being. Being is that which is

an issue for every such entity." And see also Div. I, 1, Sec. 42, p. 68: ". . . in each case 'Dasein' ist mine to be in one way or another. 'Dasein' has always made some sort of decision as to the way in which it is in each case mine ['je meines']. That entity, which in its Being has this very Being as an issue, comports itself towards its Being as its ownmost possibility." (Author's emphasis).

[265] See: Being and Time, Div. III, "The Worldhood of the World", where Heidegger explicitly stresses the need for and the importance of an investigation into the entities within the world: Things — Things of Nature, and Things "invested with value" ["wertbehaftete" Dinge]. The "Being of the Things of Nature — Nature as such" has become problematic due to the fact that its ontological meaning has been radically overlooked.

In I.3, Sec. 65, p. 93, Heidegger says in regard to this: "A glance at previous ontology shows that if one fails to see Being-in-the-world as a state of 'Dasein', the phenomenon of worldhood likewise gets passed over. One tries instead to Interpret the world in terms of the Being of those entities which are present-at-hand [vorhanden] within-the-world [innerweltlich] but which are by no means proximally discovered — namely, in terms of Nature — If one understands Nature ontologically, one finds that Nature is a limiting case of the Being of possible entities within-the-world [innerweltlich]. Only in some definite mode of its own Being-in-the-world can Dasein discover entities as Nature. This manner of knowing them has the character of depriving the world of its worldhoold in a definite way. 'Nature', as the categorial aggregate of those structures of Being which a definite entity encountered within-the-world may possess, can never make worldhood intelligible. But even the phenomenon of 'Nature', as it is conceived for instance, in romanticism, can be grasped ontologically only in terms of the concept of the world — that is to say, in terms of the analytic of 'Dasein'."

[266] In Heidegger's section of 'Being and Time' entitled "Analysis of Environmentality and Worldhood in General", the preliminary theme which he develops for "dealing . . . with entities . . . within-the-world" [innerweltlich] focuses on those entities whose concern is "with the environment". Entities of this sort are not preoccupied with theoretical knowledge of the world, but rather their natural preoccupation consists of "simply what gets used, what gets produced, and so forth". By means of this particular characterization of an aspect peculiar to 'Dasein', Heidegger clarifies the problem of "knowing the entities within-the-world" [innerweltlich] as opposed to the being of Dasein, leading in turn to a reconsideration of the 'everydayness' of being-in-the world [In-der-Welt-sein]. See Div. I,3, Secs. 67—76 (Author's emphasis).

[267] Being and Time, Div. I.6, Sec. 40, p. 228.

[268] See Heidegger's essay on "Plato's Doctrine of Truth", trans. John Barlow, in William Barret and Henry D. Aiken, Philosophy in the Twentieth Century (New York: Harper and Row, 1971), pp. 267—69.

"In Nietzsche's defining of truth as incorrectness of thinking there lies the concession to thinking of the traditional essence of truth as the correctiness of making an assertion (logos). Nietzsche's concept of truth is an example of the last reflection of the extreme consequence of that correctness of the glance. The change itself takes place in the definition of the Being of beings (i.e., according to the Greeks, the presence of what is present) as eidea. . . . In every case, man is one way or another encircled metaphysically. . . . Plato's thinking follows the change of the essence of truth, which change becomes the story of metaphysics and which has begun its unconditional fulfillment in Nietzsche's thinking."

[269] In 'Being and Time', Div. II.3, Sec. 65, 329, p. 377, Heidegger characterizes this sense of time as being "accessible to the ordinary understanding". It "consists among other things precisely in the fact that it is a pure sequence of 'nows', without beginning and without end, in which the ecstatical character of primordial temporality has been leveled off".

[270] See: Being and Time, Div. II.3, 329, p. 377. Note especially: "This very leveling off, in accordance with its existential meaning, is grounded in the possibility of a definite kind of temporalizing, in conformity with which temporalizes as inauthentic the kind of time . . . which is static.

[271] In 'Being and Time', Div. II.3, Sec. 65, 329, p. 377, Heidegger says about ecstatic time that:

"The future, the character of having been, and the Present, show the phenomenal characteristics of the towards-oneself; the back-to, and the letting-oneself-be-encountered-by, the phenomena of the 'towards . . .', the 'to' . . . and the 'alongside . . .', make temporality manifest as the 'ekstatikon' pure and simple. Temporality is the primordial outside-of-itself in and for itself. We therefore call the phenomena of the future, the character of having been, and the Present, the 'ecstatics' of temporality." (Author's emphasis).

[272] See: Being and Time, Div. II.3, 333, Sec. 66, p. 382, and also Div. II, Sec. 5, 18, p. 39, for Heidegger's critique of Bergson's conception of time.

[273] See: Heidegger, Kant and the Problem of Metaphysics, trans. James S. Churchill (Bloomington, Ind.: University of Indiana Press, 1975), pp. 166—76 and also pp. 48—54.

[274] Ibid., p. 193—201.

[275] Ibid., pp. 80—89.

[276] Ibid., pp. 188—93. Note especially, from p. 192, "Is it not evident, then, that the Kantian analysis of pure synthesis in concepts, despite the fact that it apparently has nothing to do with time, in reality reveals the most primordial essence of time, that is, that it temporalizes itself primarily out of the future?

Be that as it may, we have succeeded in showing the intrinsically temporal character of the transcendental imagination. If the transcendental imagination as the pure formative faculty in itself forms time, i.e., lets it spring forth, then the thesis stated above, that transcendental imagination is primordial time, can no longer be avoided."

[277] Ibid., pp. 106—113.

[278] For Heidegger's discussion of 'idle talk', see: Being and Time, pp. 167—170 and pp. 173—75.

[279] Ibid.

[280] In: Being and Time, Div. II.5, 168, p. 212, note especially: "In the language which is being spoken when one expresses oneself, there is an average intelligibility. . . . We do not so much understand the entities which are talked about; we already are listening only to what is said-in-talk as such. What is said-in-talk gets understood; but what the talk is about is understood only approximately and superficially."

[281] Being and Time, Div. II.1, Sec. 52, 258, p. 302.

[282] Being and Time, see Div. II.1, 246—52, especially Sec. 51.

[283] Ibid., see Div. II.1, Sec. 53.

[284] See: Being and Time, Div. II.4, Sec. 67, 340, p. 390—91.

[285] See: Being and Time, Div. II.4, p. 341—345, on fear and anxiety.

[286] Being and Time, see Div. II.3 Sec. 62.

[287] Being and Time, Div. II, Sec. 2, 298, p. 345.

[288] See: Heidegger, Time and Being, trans. Joan Stambaugh (New York: Harper and Row, 1972), p. 3.

[289] Ibid.

[290] Ibid.

[291] Ibid., p. 11.

[292] Ibid., p. 11—12.

[293] Ibid., p. 12.

[294] Ibid., p. 13.

[295] Ibid.

[296] Ibid., p. 4 (Author's emphasis).

[297] Ibid.

[298] Ibid., p. 19.

[299] Ibid., p. 21.

[300] We will merely cite two examples from his voluminous corpus in order to point to the essentially historical character of Heidegger's ontological and metaphysical investigations. In his Freiburg Lectures of 1935—36, later published in English translation as 'What Is A Thing?', Heidegger demonstrates how the answer to the question of that title is radically determined by the mathematical presuppositions of the physical sciences of each epoch which succeeds in truly asking the question embodied in the title. In particular, he examines the transformation from the physics of Aristotle to that of Descartes, Galileo, and Newton.

In 'What Is Called Thinking?' Heidegger argues that philosophic activity of the past has failed to place the nature of thought into its proper temporal context. His central theme here is that Nietzsche, taken as a paradigm, recognized the inauthentic attitude towards time which inevitably manifested itself as the nature of revenge, or the will's revulsion against the 'it was'.

[301] What remains the same from Plato to Nietzsche? See Heidegger's discussion of this problem, cited in footnote 7, P. 250.

[302] On Time and Being, p. 11.

[303] Ibid., p. 9.

[304] Ibid., p. 14.

[305] Ibid., p. 15.

[306] Ibid., pp. 15—16.

[307] Ibid., p. 14.

[308] Ibid., p. 14.

[309] Ibid., pp. 12—13.

[310] Ibid., p. 13.

[311] Ibid.

[312] Ibid.

[313] What is it that aletheia discloses? Note especially p. 259 of Heidegger's

'Plato's Doctrine of Truth': "The unhidden and its unhiddenness refer persistently to what is always openly present in the region which man abides." The *presence* of *aletheia* is not distinguished by Heidegger, as the revaluation of a '*now-point*' that has been covered over. The doctrine of *aletheia* needs to be re-thought in light of Heidegger's later discovery of the phenomenon of absence.

[314] See: "Psalm 38", New English Bible (New York: Oxford University Press, 1971).

[315] Genealogy of Morals, transl. Goffman, "Second Essay", Aphorism 1, p. 57 (My emphasis).

BIBLIOGRAPHY

Aristotle, De Anima, The Physics, The Nichomachean Ethics and Rhetoric in: The Basic Works of Aristotle. Edited by Richard McKeon. New York: Random House, 1941.

Bible, The Holy Scriptures According to the Masoretic Text, 1955, Jewish Publication Society, Philadelphia.

—, The New English. New York, Oxford University Press, 1971.

Dostoevsky, Fyodor, The Brothers Karamazov. Translated by Constance Garnett. (The Modern Library.) New York: Random House, 1950.

—, Notes from the Underground. Translated by Constance Garnett. Revised and Edited by Avraham Yarmolinsky. Garden City, New York: Anchor Books, Doubleday & Co., 1960.

Heidegger, Martin, Being and Time. Translated by John Macquarrie and Edward Robinson, from 'Sein und Zeit' (1927), 7th ed. London: SCM Press, 1962.

—, Kant and the Problem of Metaphysics. Translated by James S. Churchill from 'Kant und das Problem der Metaphysik' (1927). Bloomington and London: Indiana University Press, 1975.

—, An Introduction to Metaphysics. Translated by Ralph Manheim, from 'Einführung in die Metaphysik' (1935). New Haven, Conn.: Yale University Press, 1959.

—, On Time and Being. Translated by Joan Stambaugh from "Zeit und Sein" (1962). New York: Harper and Row, 1972.

—, "Plato's Doctrine of Truth". Translated by John Barlow from 'Platons Lehre von der Wahrheit' (1942). In: Philosophy in the Twentieth Century. Edited by William Barret and Henry D. Aiken. New York: Torchbooks, Harper and Row, 1971.

—, What Is A Thing?. Translated by W. B. Barton, Jr., and Vera Deutsch from 'Die Frage Nach dem Ding' (1962). Chicago: Henry Regnery Company, 1967.

—, What is Called Thinking?. Translated by Fred Wieck and J. Glenn Gray from 'Was heißt Denken?' (1951). New York: Harper and Row, 1968.

—, "Who is Nietzsche's Zarathustra?", translated by Bernd Magnus from 'Wer ist Nietzsches Zarathustra' (1953). In: The Review of Metaphysics, XX 91967).

Homer, The Iliad. Translated by E. V. Rieu. Middlesex, England: Penguin Books, 1950.

Kaufmann, Walter, ed., Existentialism from Dostoevsky to Sartre. New York: World Publishing Co., 1972.

Kaufmann, Walter, Nietzsche. New York: Vintage Books, Alfred A. Knopf and Random House, 1968.

Levinas, Emmanuel, Totality and Infinity. Translated by Alphonso Lingis from 'Totalite e Infini'. Pittsburgh: Duquesne University Press; The Hague: Martinis Nijhoff, 1969.

Magnus, Bernd, Heidegger's Metahistory of Philosophy. The Hague: Martinus Nighoff, 1970.

Mochulsky, Konstantin, Dostoevksy: His Life and Work. Translated by Michael A. Minihan. Princeton: Princeton University Press, 1967.

Nietzsche, Friedrich, "The Antichrist". Translated by Walter Kaufmann from 'Der Antichrist' (1888; first published 1895) in: The Portable Nietzsche.

—, Basic Writings of Nietzsche (includes: The Birth of Tragedy, "Seventy-five Aphorisms", Beyond Good and Evil, On the Genealogy of Morals, The Case of Wagner, and Ecce Homo). Translated by Walter Kaufmann. New York: Random House, 1968.

—, The Birth of Tragedy. Translated by Walter Kaufmann from 'Der Geburt der Tragödie' (1872). New York: Random House, 1967.

—, Ecce Homo, Translated by Walter Kaufmann from 'Ecce Homo' (1888) in: The Portable Nietzsche.

—, On the Genealogy of Morals. Translated by Walter Kaufmann and R. J. Hollingdale from 'Zur Genealogie der Moral' (1887). New York: Random House, 1967.

—, Philosophy in the Tragic Age of the Greeks. Translated by Mary Ann Cowan from 'Die Philosophie im tragischen Zeitalter der Griechen' (ca. 1872). Chicago: Henry Regnery Co., 1962.

—, The Portable Nietzsche (includes: Twilight of the Idols, The Antichrist, Nietzsche contra Wagner, and Thus Spoke Zarathustra). Translated by Walter Kaufmann. New York: Viking, 1968.

—, Thus Spoke Zarathustra. Translated by Walter Kaufmann from 'Also Sprach Zarathustra' (1883—1885) in: The Portable Nietzsche.

—, Twilight of the Idols. Translated by Walter Kaufmann from 'Die Götzen-Dämmerung' (1889) in: The Portable Nietzsche.

—, The Will to Power. Translated by Walter Kaufmann and R. J. Hollingdale from 'Der Wille zur Macht' (variously edited and published since 1901). New York: Vintage, 1968.

Plato, 'Symposium' and 'Euthyphro' in particular. In: The Collected Dialogues of Plato. Edited by Edith Hamilton and Huntington Cairns. (Bollingen Series LXXI.) Princeton: Princeton University Press, 1963.

Scheler, Max, On the Eternal in Man. Translated by Bernard Noble from 'Vom Ewigen im Menschen' (1920). London Camelot Press; SCM Press, 1960.

—, Ressentiment. Translated by W. Holdheim. Edited by L. Coser. New York: The Free Press of Glencoe, 1961.
    Scheler's 'Ressentiment' originally appeared under the title of "Über Ressentiment und moralisches Werturteil" in: Zeitschrift für Pathopsychologie, Jahrg. I. H. 2/3. Leipzig: Verlag Engelmann, 1912. It was republished in its final, extended form under the new title "Das Ressentiment im Aufbau der Moralen", in: Gesammelte Abhandlungen und Aufsätze. The Holdheim translation is based on the fourth edition of 'Vom Umsturz der Werte', edited by Maria Scheler, published as Volume III of Max Scheler's 'Gesammelte Werke'. Bern: Francke Verlag.

Shakespeare, William, Macbeth. In: The Complete Signet Classic Shakespeare. Edited by Sylvan Barret. New York: New American Library, 1974.

Solomon, Robert, ed., Nietzsche: A Collection of Critical Essays. Garden City, New York: Anchor Books, Doubleday & Co., 1970.

Stambaugh, Joan, Nietzsche's Thought of Eternal Return. Baltimore and London: Johns Hopkins University Press, 1972.

VIII. INDEX

AUTHOR'S NOTE

The tradition of phenomenology in America was guided for a generation by John Wild with whom it was my privilege to have studied for eight years. He wanted me to write a phenomenology of promise, and work had only begun on that project when, in an way this book shows, the phenomenon of 'ressentiment' presented itself as an existential impediment to an authentic articulation of a philosophy of promise. While the phenomenology of 'ressentiment' makes good on one promise, it marks the beginning of another.

I have been the beneficiary of much encouragement, good counsel, and timely support in the preparation of this book. Erazim Kohak and Bernard Elevitch of Boston University provided invaluable criticism and good will during the time that the substance of this manuscript was prepared. My two constant companions in philosophy, Robert J. Anderson and Roger B. Duncan proved that their mentor Plato was right in maintaining that the best of friends are philosophers. To my friend Kaye Schmucker who taught me that writing is something that becomes, I am most grateful. To Cynthia Regas, my devoted student, who kept track of every page of every draft, and every footnote on every page, I am most indebted.

To Helen Stephenson, Dawn Lawrence, and Kathleen Gunther who assisted in the typing and preparation of this manuscript under conditions that were often trying, I am most appreciative.

I wish to reserve a special word of thanks to my friends David Meltzer, William Roth, and R. Thomas Simone who have provided me with constant encouragement in my work in philosophy over the course of many years. Lastly, to my beloved friend the late Rabbi Shmuel Heckt who showed me that there is always promise even when the time is short, I remain eternally grateful.

Philosophische Bibliothek

These green volumes offer an easy access to scholarly yet usuable philosophical texts and are an indispensable aid to the study of philosophy the world over. The series includes more than 150 critical editions, some of them bilingual. The following list of authors represents a selection: Bolzano, Brentano, Fichte, Frege, Hegel, Herder, Husserl, Kant, Leibniz, L. Nelson, Nicolas Cusanus, Reinhold, Schelling, Schleiermacher, Schopenhauer, Tetens, Thomas Aquinas.

Felix Meiner is also reponsible for the following editions:

G. W. F. Hegel, Gesammelte Werke

Four volumes have so far appeared, another six are in the process of being printed. "The book (volume 4 / Jenaer kritische Schriften) is magnificently produced . . . The book is a pleasure to read and to study. It is of course indispensable for all libraries that care for scholarship, as well as for all serious students of Hegel". (T. M. Knox, University of St. Andrews)

Nicolai de Cusa, Opera omnia

Fifteen volumes have appeared, three further volumes are in preparation. The more important texts are available as bilingual study-editions. Still to appear are the **Acta Cusana**, source-material of the life of Nicolas Cusanus, planned as nine fascicles. One has appeared.

Leonard Nelson, Gesammelte Schriften in neun Bänden

L. Nelson (1882—1927) is considered as a reciver of the critical philosophy inaugurated and elaborated by I. Kant, J. F. Fries, and E. F. Apelt.

Gottlob Frege, Nachgelassene Schriften und Wissenschaftlicher Briefwechsel

"Frege's manuskripts help deepen to and expand one's picture of one of the most significant figures in the history of logic." (Journal of Philosophy)

Dietrich von Freiberg, Opera omnia

The edition contains in four volumes all 25 manuscript treatises so far traced to this original late mediaeval thinker (1250—1310), who is of vital importance for the history of philosophy, theology and science. Supplemantary volumes (**Beihefte**) are planned.

If you wish your name to be added to our mailing list, please write to us. Our catalogue will be sent to you twice a year.

FELIX MEINER VERLAG

Richardstraße 47 · D-2000 Hamburg 76 · Federal Republic of Germany